TALES OF GLORY

with Riley K. Smith

India: Tales of Glory

VOM Books
P.O. Box 443
Bartlesville, OK 74005-0443

Previously published by Living Sacrifice Books, an imprint of The Voice of the Martyrs.

ISBN 978-0-88264-032-7

Edited by Lynn Copeland

Cover design by Lookout Design

Cover creation, page design, and layout by Genesis Group

Printed in the United States of America

Unless otherwise indicated, Scripture references are from the *New King James* version, © 1979, 1980, 1982 by Thomas Nelson Inc., Publishers, Nashville, Tennessee.

THE TRUE HEROES:
OR, THE NOBLE ARMY OF MARTYRS

You who love a tale of glory,
Listen to the song I sing;
Heroes of the Christian story,
Are the heroes I shall bring.

Warriors of the world, avaunt!
Other heroes me engage;
'Tis not such as you I want,
Saints and martyrs grace my page.

Fearful Christian! hear with wonder,
Of the saints of whom I tell;
Some were burnt, some sawn asunder,
Some by fire or torture fell;

Martyrs who were thus arrested,
In their short but bright career;
By their blood the truth attested,
Proved their faith and love sincere.

Though their lot was hard and lowly,
Though they perish'd at the stake,
Now they live with Christ in glory,
Since they suffer'd for his sake.

Fierce and unbelieving foes
But their bodies could destroy;
Short, though bitter, were their woes,
Everlasting is their joy.

—HANNAH MORE (1745–1833), English evangelical
writer and philanthropist

*"The Christian road in India has always
been an uphill road."*
—STEPHEN NEILL,
A History of Christianity in India

INDIA

CONTENTS

ACKNOWLEDGMENTS

Thank you, Margot A., for loaning me your copy of *A Memorial of the Futtehgurh Mission and Her Martyred Missionaries*, uncovering information on the Great Mutiny that I was searching for. Many thanks to David Hepworth for your diligence in tracking down photos, maps, and other images for this book. Your cartographical skills are appreciated! To my peer reviewers, Todd Nettleton and one other who must remain nameless, your careful reading and thoughtful evaluations sharpen and complete the message of these Restricted Nations books. To the copyeditor, Lynn Copeland, whose enduring passion for truth and accuracy never cease to make me smile with yet another opportunity to refine the focus and enhance the clarity of the book's message. To my friends and family who prayed for this book during each stage of its development.

Finally, to my brothers and sisters in India who dare to turn from their ancient religion of Hinduism in search of a God who views all His children equal...and pay dearly for doing so! I look forward to meeting you in eternity!

May this book inspire many to pray for and assist India's suffering saints. And may this book inspire those in the free world to run their race well...and hard (Habakkuk 2:2)!

BEFORE THE TALE BEGINS...

They came from the steppes of Russia, driven out of their land of birth. As the Aryans took up their meager belongings, they drove their herds and conquered the peoples that stood in their way. Some gradually migrated eastward and settled in the land we know today as India. And they brought with them their gods and goddesses, setting the country on a course that would plague the people for centuries—and millennia—to come.

What little we know of the Aryans comes from a collection of verses, poems, prayers, and instructions called the Vedas, which were passed down orally through the ages. The most important and earliest written of the Vedas is the Rig Veda, with hymns to the Aryans' various gods and goddesses. Composed about 1500 B.C., it was put in writing sometime after 300 B.C. And it is these writings that became the foundation of the religion followed by more than eighty percent of Indians today—Hinduism.

An Indefinable Religion

India's Supreme Court declared it complicated, if not impossible, to define or even adequately explain. It doesn't claim any one prophet, and it doesn't worship one God. It has no single orthodoxy, or a set of beliefs that all its followers *must* adhere to. And it does not follow any one set of religious rites or ceremonies.

This is Hinduism—the world's third largest religion.

One expert says that Hinduism "has ever aimed at accommodating itself to circumstances and has carried on the process of adaptation through more than three thousand years. It has ...swallowed, digested, and assimilated something from all creeds."[1] Even the *Encyclopedia Britannica* admits, "Every attempt at a specific definition of Hinduism has proved unsatisfactory in one way or another, the more so because the finest Indian scholars of Hinduism, including Hindus themselves, have emphasized different aspects of that religion."

And India's Supreme Court determined that "no precise meaning can be ascribed to...Hinduism; and no meaning in the abstract can confine it to the narrow limits of religion alone, excluding the content of Indian culture and heritage."

What many scholars and experts *will* agree upon are some basic core beliefs.

Central to Hinduism is the belief in an ultimate reality called *Brahman*. To the Hindu, the human soul (*jiva*) is everlasting and in a perpetual state of development through successive lifetimes, called reincarnation. After death, the soul is born again on earth into a new bodily form with the purpose of bettering itself and eventually becoming one with Brahman. This rebirth is gov-

---

1 Monier-Williams, p. 57.

erned by *kharma*, the law of moral consequences. Therefore, to the Hindu, what a person was and did in a past life will dictate his place in the present life.

It is this set of core beliefs that formed the basis of India's caste system, which, according to some missionaries to India, has been one of the biggest obstacles to the gospel, and today is one of the factors behind why Christians are persecuted. But how did it get this way?

The Hindu Social Order

Described as "India's apartheid," a failed attempt at a "social utopia," and "enslaving," Hindu's caste system rapidly developed into four social categories—a hierarchy—well before the birth of Christ.

At the top of the caste are the *Brahmins*, who claim to be born from the mouth of God. Next are the *Kshatriyas*, born from the arms of God, followed by the *Vaishyas* from God's belly. And finally, there are the *Shudras*, who are from God's feet. Then there are those without caste, called *Dalits*, or "untouchables." This visual and its terms alone depict how Hindus, especially Brahmins, view those of lower castes—or no caste. No caste means no status. But by the beginning of the twentieth century, the caste system multiplied exponentially into more than two thousand different castes in India.

To Hindus, the caste system means everyone has their defined place and function in society.

However, such segmentation is based on a belief that God created man unequal—a belief that defies the biblical view.

With the arrival of the gospel message to India our tale begins, and it starts with an apostle who challenged a group of Brahmins—a challenge that cost him his life.

THOMAS' TALE: THE GOSPEL ARRIVES (1ST CENTURY)

It wasn't enough that the other disciples had seen Jesus.

"He's alive, Thomas!" they announced. "We have seen Him!"

One can imagine the sneer that dampened the disciples' excitement when they heard Thomas' response.

"Unless I see the print of the nails in His hands, and put my finger into them and into His side," Thomas insisted, "I will not believe."

With those words, Thomas became labeled throughout Christian history, forever bearing the title "Doubting Thomas."

Eight days later, Jesus appeared again to the disciples. This time, He looked straight at this skeptic and said, "Reach your finger here, and look at My hands; and reach your hand here, and put it into My side. Do not be unbelieving, but believing."

Finally convinced, Thomas cried out, "My Lord and my God!"

Jesus returned to heaven, and according to tradition, the disciples divided the regions of the known world among them to evangelize. For Thomas, the lot fell to India.

This is where our tale of Thomas taking the gospel to India comes to a crossroads.

One tradition, called the *Acts of Thomas*, was penned by a Christian in Edessa around the year A.D. 200. In what some scholars consider an exaggerated account, his telling claimed that Thomas fiercely opposed going to India, defending his title as a "Doubter."

"I am a Hebrew man; how can I go among the Indians and preach the truth?" Thomas argued.

As he justified his decision, this same tradition tells the story that Jesus appeared to him that night and said, "Fear not, Thomas, go to India and preach the word, for My grace is with you."

Still, Thomas wouldn't go. This time Jesus intervened.

Jesus appeared to a merchant named Abbanes, who was visiting Jerusalem to procure a slave to build King Gundaphores' palace. Jesus brokered the deal. Thomas was the slave. Thomas finally gave in to India and left with Abbanes.

When they arrived in northern India, the king is said to have instructed Thomas on the palace plan, gave Thomas the funds he needed to begin, and then left.

Seeing the poor and destitute around him, Thomas used the money to help them, instead of buying building materials and labor. The king returned only to discover that Thomas had not laid a single stone.

When the king asked Thomas when he would see the palace, the apostle replied, "You cannot see it now, but when you leave this life, then you will see it."

The king was furious and threw Thomas in prison but later released him. In this tradition, Thomas traveled India until he met his end. After he led a family member of King Misdaeus to Christ, the angry king ordered his execution.

Indian tradition, on the other hand, takes a more willing and non-enslaved Thomas to the subcontinent. Indian tradition claims that he arrived in India in the south where he founded churches, helping thousands turn to Christ. This tradition says that Thomas met his end after a confrontation with Brahmin priests near Pelayur in Kerala.

A group of Nambudiri Brahmins[2] were performing a cleansing ritual in the water of a temple basin. Thomas watched them as they tossed water into the air while chanting their prayers.

"Why are you doing that?" asked Thomas.

"It is our sacrifice to the gods," they replied.

"Then why aren't your gods accepting it?" asked Thomas. He couldn't resist the opportunity to challenge them as he humorously observed that the water drops kept falling back on them.

Annoyed, the Brahmins returned the challenge. "Who can make the water stay up in the air?"

---

2 Nambudiri Brahmins are from the Indian state of Kerala and are considered the most orthodox Brahmins in India. Members regard themselves as the true "keepers" of the ancient Vedic religion and of the traditional Hindu code.

"I can," claimed Thomas.

Surely the Brahmins found this strange-looking man with lighter skin and a long nose a fool. "Prove it!"

"Only if you promise to be baptized if I succeed," replied Thomas.

The Brahmin priests couldn't resist. They agreed to the deal. How could they lose? They would prove this arrogant foreigner wrong.

Thomas walked up to the basin, cupped the cool water in his hands, and tossed it up into the air. The Brahmins also looked up into the blue sky, anticipating their win.

But there was no water.

According to this tradition, the water droplets never returned to the earth. They were caught in the reflection of the sun and sparkled like diamonds.

Refusing their end of the deal, the Brahmins demanded that Thomas worship the Hindu goddess Kali. Thomas refused. As he made the sign of the cross, the grove where the priests had gathered burst into flames, perhaps as an act demonstrating God's might over Kali, the Hindu goddess of destruction.

Thomas' end was sealed. The Brahmins determined that he must die. They pierced him with a stake at Mylapore around A.D. 70.

And ever since then, Christians in southwest India have dubbed themselves "Thomas Christians," with this tale being passed down orally through songs and poems.

* * *

Once a skeptic, now a hero. And Thomas' tale is not only told in India today. It is also lived out as countless Indians have chosen to follow Christ and take His Great Commission seriously.

The pages you are about to read are full of such tales of Christian courage throughout India's history to today. Like Thomas, some were persecuted at the hands of Brahmins, others by Muslim occupiers, and many by their own countrymen. There was even a time in India's history that a

The martyrdom of the apostle Thomas

Western power hindered the spread of the gospel on the subcontinent.

As you read, may their tales of glory encourage you to partake in the grace promised to those who choose to go wherever Christ leads! And may they inspire you to partake in their race.

INDIA TODAY:
THE PLEDGE

They came to receive their diplomas. But that wasn't enough for the fifteen hundred graduates of Emmanuel Theological Seminary and Bible College in Kota, Rajasthan. What they learned at the college would cost them greatly, so before their peers and professors, they made this pledge:

I stand with the apostle Paul in stating that "for me to live is Christ and to die is gain."

I take a stand to honor the Lord Jesus Christ with my hands to serve all mankind.

I take a stand to honor the Lord Jesus Christ with my feet to spread the gospel to all the ends of the earth no matter what the cost.

I take a stand to honor the Lord Jesus Christ with my lips by proclaiming the Good News to all who hear and by edifying the Body of Christ.

I take a stand to honor the Lord Jesus Christ with my mind as I meditate upon His Word and His promises to me.

I give my earthly treasures and all that I possess to follow the way of the cross.

I commit to love my family, orphans, widows, lepers, the wealthy and the poor the way that Christ loved the church.

I surrender my will and life to His will and life.

I commit to the service of the Lord by being a good steward of my time.

I surrender this body on earth to the perfect will of Jesus, and should my blood be spilled may it bring forth a mighty harvest of souls.

I pledge allegiance to the Lamb. I will seek to honor His command. I am not ashamed of the gospel of Christ, for it is the power of God unto salvation to everyone who believes.

Lord Jesus, Thy Kingdom come. Thy will be done on earth as it is in heaven.

I love my India and my fellow citizens, and I claim India for Christ.

At the ceremony was a new Christian who returned to his village to share the gospel only to face hostility. Villagers tied old shoes around his neck and forced him to parade down the street as they beat him. That wasn't enough for the villagers. They made him drink cow urine. But what happened next was not what the villagers had hoped: his courageous witness caused a hundred villagers to turn to Christ.

Two years after composing this pledge, a militant Hindu mob assaulted more than two hundred fifty Emmanuel students on their way to their graduation in Kota. Police took the wounded students to the station where they were once again beaten, this time with iron rods and bicycle chains. Now with all their possessions taken from them, they were forced to return home. Still, more than four thousand students came from across India to graduate.

For many, their diplomas have been sealed with suffering as they take the gospel into a society increasingly hostile to Christ. Radical Hindus have taken up arms to make India a purely Hindu state, calling any other religion, like Christianity and even Islam, a foreign invasion.

Blood will be spilled as Christians in India pledge to preach Christ and Him crucified. But the glory is found in the words of the early church leader Tertullian: "The blood of the martyrs is the seed of the church." The harvest of souls is and will continue to be forthcoming!

COPPER PLATES, CROSSES, AND CLUES: THE 2ND CENTURY TO THE ARRIVAL OF CATHOLICS

"The people persecute much the Christians and all who bear the Christian name."

—JOHN OF MONTECORVINO, 1291

The tale of Thomas' arrival and martyrdom soon spread. Poems, songs, and even the allegedly embellished account of his life were penned and passed on to the next generation. Word got out about Thomas as merchants were coming and going on the subcontinent, now experiencing its golden age as its spices, jewels, and other material luxuries were sought for profit.

Thomas' martyrdom faintly foreshadowed the fate of Christians in the centuries that followed his death. First of all, Thomas wasn't martyred in a mass government-sanctioned persecution of Christians as the apostle Paul was by Nero. And neither did his martyrdom ignite mass persecution at the hands of religious zealots, like Stephen's in the Book of Acts. Thomas was martyred, buried, and since then remembered in the traditions by those who have identified themselves as "Thomas Christians." And what history has to say in the form of brief accounts and references to persecution has, unfortunately, rendered the details more of a mystery.

A Nasrani Menorah (Mar Thoma Cross), symbolic of St. Thomas Christians' long history in India

Reliable written records of Christians in India trace back no further than the eighth or ninth century, and even these are still subject to interpretation. The most important are the Kerala copper plates, which contain the earliest details of the Christian community in India. The other evidence is found in five stone "St. Thomas" crosses in south India, shedding very little light on the ancient Christians.

Neither the copper plates nor crosses seem to allude to any further martyrdom or persecution of Christians. However, there are some shreds of evidence from history that do give us a glimpse.

Palm Leaves and Letters

A manuscript entitled "The Affairs of Christianity in Kerala," written on a palm leaf[3] dating to early nineteenth century, provides a clue to India's persecuted past. It says that in A.D. 293, Christians were being persecuted in "the rest of" India, causing many to flee to Malabar. In "The Puhur City of Cavery River," the king was persecuting the Christians, so seventy-two families boarded a ship for Kollam.

---

3 Dried palm leaves served as paper in parts of Asia until the arrival of printing presses in the early nineteenth century.

Almost twenty years later, a sorcerer went to Kollam and forced to convert back to Hinduism more than a hundred people belonging to eight of the seventy-two families that had fled there. Other Christians were also targeted in the forced re-conversion—a practice that takes place in India today. Some historians question the credibility of the re-conversion segment of the story.

Evidence indicates that Persian Christians also immigrated to India when they were persecuted in their homeland. During Persia's Great Persecution (A.D. 340–401), those Christians who managed to avoid Shah Shapur II's carnage fled to India. One merchant named Thomas of Cana landed on the Malabar Coast. Hundreds of people traveled with him, including Nestorian[4] deacons, priests, and bishops. They, too, met the Christians who traced their origin to Thomas.

Missionaries and merchants continued arriving around the fourth century during the Gupta dynasty (A.D. 319–500), when the society at large was predominately Hindu and caste rose in importance with a great emphasis on Brahmin purity. The Hindu temple became the focus of social

---

4 The fifth century witnessed a rift between the churches in the East and West. It began when a theologian named Nestorius criticized a well-known religious expression, erupting into a conflict regarding Christ the person and Christ the divine. Nestorius was condemned for his beliefs at the Council of Ephesus in A.D. 431. Adding to the controversy was Nestorius' claim that he rejected the divine nature of Christ ("God the Word") was capable of suffering.

and religious life, and images were worshiped. As Hindus visited the temples to pay homage to the gods and goddesses, the temple coffers grew with donated treasures. It's possible that such a focus on Hinduism may have attributed to more attacks on Christians in isolated areas of India, especially those who left Hinduism.

From 850 to 1250, little is known of the church, with some referring to this time as the "silent centuries." Marco Polo makes a brief reference to the Christians in Quilon. Catholic missionary John of Montecorvino arrived in India in 1291 to visit the burial site of Thomas. He stayed thirteen months. He wrote of the Thomas Christians and even mentioned persecution: "There are very few Christians and Jews and they are of little weight. The people persecute much the Christians and all who bear the Christian name."

No mention was made of how or why they suffered, just that they were persecuted...even for having a Christian name. We can assume that such persecution occurred when a monotheistic faith (Christianity) came into conflict with a polytheistic religion (Hinduism). And when a Hindu turned to Christ, any high-caste standing was presumably lost.

Hindus would soon face another rival in the faith—Islam, which began to arrive on the subcontinent in the seventh century. Once it began to take root, more suffering came to both Christians and Hindus.

BORDERS BREACHED: ISLAM HITS THE SUBCONTINENT (7TH–16TH CENTURIES)

They were desert nomads of the Arabian Peninsula, now united under one religion and with one purpose: to bring the world under subjection to Islam—the *Dar-al-Islam*.

As early as the seventh century, Arab invaders chanted "*Allahu-Akbar*" ("God is great") as they swept through the Near East, subjecting empires to its dogma: "There is no god but Allah, and Mohammed is his prophet." Persia fell to the invaders whose message was more political and militant than religious. Their demands were to either convert to Islam, or face death or subjection to the *dhimma*—a treaty of compliance with minority religions in a country conquered by Islam.

Jews, Christians, and followers of other religions found themselves faced with risking death when proclaiming their faith or surviving under the *dhimma* when keeping their faith to themselves. Those under the *dhimma* paid a very high poll tax, called a *jizya*, which supported Islam's military and administration.

India would face Islam's sword but not until the end of the seventh century.

Dhimma and Disgruntled Masses

India felt the brunt of the Arabs' sword toward the end of the seventh century as Muslims invaded portions of the subcontinent. For some reason, the invaders stopped at the city of Sind in north-west India (in today's Pakistan) and went no further. Apparently at this stage in history, Arabs were more interested in India's wealth than subjecting the people to their religion.

Decades later, when Muhammed ibn Qasim invaded Sind, he showed no mercy and demanded the Brahmins be circumcised or face death.

Qasim, realizing the rising repugnance among the "infidel Hindus," instead invoked the *dhimma* and imposed the hated *jizya* tax on all those who chose to adhere to a faith other than Islam. However, the Muslims were too few to confine a disgruntled people to the *dhimma* or to enact some form of persecution against those who chose to live outside their alleged rights. Some Hindus did convert to Islam, especially those of lower castes who saw the conversion to Islam as a means of escape from their perceived bad *kharma*.

In the centuries that followed, Arab Muslim invaders came and went, until the tenth century when Turkish Muslims breached India's borders.

The Sultanates

They overturned the Byzantine Empire and conquered Asia Minor, but that wasn't enough for the Turkish Muslims who set their sights on India.

Around 977, Mahmoud of Gazna launched seventeen ruthless raids in India. He targeted the temple cities of northern India that housed incalculable treasures of gold, silver, jewels, and precious stones, all donated by Hindu worshipers. But the temples also housed great abominations to the Allah-chanting assailants—Hindu idols.

Mahmoud continued his rampage in the early eleventh century, and by the end of his reign, Punjab had become a part of his empire and Islam became well-rooted in northwest India. (To this day Islam remains there.)

However, unlike Persia and Egypt, Islam failed to take root in the rest of India. Some say that to the Indian rulers, the Islamic invaders were just another foreign aggressor, like the Sakas and Huns of Central Asia in previous centuries. The Muslim invaders also never fully integrated into India's complex cultural framework. They remained a separate religion and culture and to this day maintain their own rituals and customs. Eventually, a portion of India's northwest would break off and create its own independent country, but not for almost a millennium.

With Mahmoud's death, Islam's threat dwindled, but Muhammad of Ghur would take up the cause and continue the Turkish onslaught until the city of Delhi finally fell in 1202. Bengal was also crushed, as well as Orissa, Assam, and Bihar. Bihar witnessed the complete destruction of Buddhist monasteries and the massacre of Buddhist monks, wiping Buddhism off its homeland[5] for good. (Today less than one percent follows Buddhism in India.)

Muhammad of Ghur's assassination in 1206 ushered in the Delhi sultanate, in which Turks ruled for more than three hundred years. The Delhi sultanate later tried expanding the kingdom to India's south, but its policies caused economic and social animosity leading to dissent and conflict. In the meantime, Bengal gave its allegiance to Delhi in 1338 and created its own separate Muslim kingdom but not before the Hindu kingdom of Vijayanagar was founded and in the next two centuries expanded its influence from coast to coast.

Still, India was invaded in the north. The savage Mongol militant Tamerlane captured Delhi. His men so destroyed the city that it was deserted for almost a hundred years.

During the fifteenth century, independent sultanates appeared in west and central India. From what history tells us, those Christians who

---

5 Buddhism was founded by the Indian prince Siddhartha Gautama, who lived circa 563–483 B.C. Having lived a sheltered life, Siddhartha ventured outside the palace walls where he soon became aware of society's suffering. Unable to find the answers to life's problems in Hindu scriptures, he turned to meditation, during which he concluded that desire is the root of all human suffering and developed Buddhism's basic tenets: the Four Noble Truths and the Eightfold Path.

link their origins to Thomas did not suffer much as regions of India were ransacked and ruined. Historians say that what is known of the Thomas Christians at this time exists in "separated fragments and small clusters, which accentuate silence of evidence." Brief and general references to Christian persecution made by those passing through the country are recorded, such as the story of the four Franciscans martyred at the hands of a fanatical Muslim.

STORY FROM HISTORY: THE FOUR FRANCISCANS

Their destination was China, but the four missionaries first stopped in India to visit the church of St. Thomas at Mylapore.

The year was 1320, and Thomas de Tolentino, James of Padua, Peter of Sienna, and their translator Demetrius of Tiftis had set sail from the Persian Gulf. As their ship pushed through the deep waters, a violent storm forced their vessel to shore near Bombay. A group of Nestorians took the sea-soaked missionaries to their town, Tana, and found them a place to stay. But the town's hospitality would be short-lived.

A woman in Tana launched a complaint against her husband, and the four Franciscans were called upon to bear witness in the case. But the four were likely surprised when the Qadi, the Muslim judge in the community, did not ask them questions about the case.

"What do you think of Mohammed?" asked the Qadi, who directed the question at Thomas.

"Mohammed is an imposter, and those who believe in him will certainly follow him to hell," replied Thomas without a thought to the effects his terse words would have on the stern black-haired judge before him.

The Qadi was furious. *How dare he blaspheme the prophet!* He used threats to coerce Thomas into refuting his profane proclamations against

Mohammed. He tried to bribe Thomas to apologize for what he had said.

But Thomas refused, and none of the Franciscans gave the Qadi any indication that they would try to convince Thomas to change his mind. Perhaps Thomas' resolve came from the fact that he was already well-acquainted with suffering for his beliefs. Years earlier he had been imprisoned in Europe for his extreme Franciscan views of absolute poverty.

Seeing the four men unshaken by his threats and refusing to deny Christ and convert to Islam, the Qadi decided to take a different approach with the infidels.

The Qadi's men tore off the Franciscans' robes and tied them to posts to endure the burning sun. Hours later, instead of begging for relief, the men stood singing praises to the Lord as their light skin blistered in the blazing rays. Incensed, the Qadi had to silence them for good and ordered that they perish by the sword.

But their death wasn't the end of the tale.

One night as the Qadi slept, he had a dream of the Franciscans demanding he treat Christians more compassionately. Apparently, the martyred foursome weren't the only believers that the Qadi was persecuting.

Alarmed by his dream, he awoke the next morning and released all Christians from prison, called back those who had been banished, and even issued a public edict forbidding anyone who insulted a follower of Christ. As a result, a great number of Muslims and idol worshipers turned to Christ.

The four Franciscans never made it to China to preach the gospel. Instead, they laid down their lives in India, where their glorious witness caused a Qadi's change of heart and many villagers to turn to Christ.

PEPPER AND THE POPE:
THE PORTUGUESE ARRIVAL
(1498–EARLY 18TH CENTURY)

With a cross on his banner and a missionary on his ship, Vasco da Gama embarked on the ten-month journey from Lisbon, Portugal, to India. Muslims dominated the seas through the Middle East. And after an embarrassing defeat for the church in the Crusades, another confrontation with the Turks and Arabs was something to be avoided.

So when Calicut, India, came into da Gama's sight after sailing around the continent of Africa, he knew he struck gold in the form of spices, silks, and precious jewels. He also discovered another treasure: Christians.

Discovering an Ancient Church
The Thomas Christians, who traced their origins to the apostle, welcomed da Gama and his men and even showed him the chapel at Mylapore where Thomas was believed to be buried. The Thomas Christians hoped the Portuguese would be their liberators, bringing an end to the caste discrimination imposed on them by the Hindu rulers. Likewise, the Hindu rulers hoped the Portuguese would align themselves against the Muslim invaders that crept in from the north. In reality, the Portuguese had other plans.

Ernesto Casanova's painting of Vasco da Gama. He arrived in India in 1498.

Disappointed that the Thomas Christians didn't control the lucrative pepper trade, the Portuguese drove out the Muslim traders and employed the Thomas Christians, who had worked in agriculture. As the ships kept coming from Portugal on their newfound route around Africa, so did Portuguese missionaries. But these messengers of hope soon learned that these Christians did not answer to the pope; they answered to a

Nestorian patriarch in Persia. In the decades that followed, the missionaries would try to "latinize" the Thomas Christians, ensuring loyalty to the pope and enforcing Catholic customs. Unfortunately, this would backfire and wouldn't serve to empower the church but riddle it with conflict.

Still, the Portuguese were amazed at how well established this ancient church was, especially surviving under both Hindu rulers and Muslim invaders from the north. However, their survival came at a price, as some incorporated Hindu rituals and "ordeals"[6] into their daily lives. In one part of India, the Thomas Christians had to pay a ruler for their protection and recognize him as their defender and protector.

Colonies and Conversion
Almost ten years after da Gama's arrival, the Portuguese established their colonies. They built a hospital on the coast of Conchin and a school for Christian children, mixing low and high castes, which did not please the local Hindus. Those Indians who converted to the religion of the new foreign inhabitants were immediately considered outcastes by the Hindus. Ironically, those who converted to Islam did not face the same discrimination.

---

6 Ordeals are what a modern-day Westerner would call "extreme" dares. These included touching red-hot irons, putting one's hand into a pot of burning oil, and swimming across a river full of crocodiles.

The Portuguese spread into the coastal cities of India, setting up ports to ship spices and other goods from India. First they took Goa, then Malacca and Ormuz. But still, the Red Sea remained in the hands of their Muslim rivals. As the Portuguese established their colonial settlements, it wasn't long before they offended the local Hindus.

To a Hindu, only those of lower castes (or no caste) ate meat, and the Portuguese loved eating meat. Therefore, Christianity was quickly associ-

EUROPEAN SETTLEMENTS IN INDIA
(1501-1739)

TIBET

PAKISTAN

NEPAL

INDIA

Arabian Sea

■▦ (1537)
▦ (1658) Hughli
■ ▮ (1675) Chandernagar
▦ (1675) Serampore
▦ (1690) Calcutta

Chinsu

Surat (1612) ▦
Daman (1558) ■▮

■▮ (1535) Diu

Bassein [Baçaim] (1533) ■▮
Bombay (1638) ▦

Bay of Be

Vizagapatam (1682) ▦

LEGEND
▦ British Settlements
▦ Danish Settlements
▭ Dutch Settlements
▮▮ French Settlements
■▮ Portuguese Settlements

Goa (1610) ■▮

Yanam (1725) ▮▮

Masulipatam (1616) ▭

Pulicat (1600) ▭
▦ (1639) Madras
Sadras (1670) ▭
Pondicherry (1674) ▮▮
Karikal (1739) ▮▮
Nagapatam (1507) ■▮ (1658) ▭
Jaffna (1658) ▭

■▮ (1501) Carinanora
▮▮ (1725) Mahe
■▮ (1498) Calicut
■▮ (1500) Cochin
▮▮ (1669)

Tranquebar
▦ (1620)

Trincomale (1522) ■▮
(1639) (1674) ▭
(1673) ▮▮

■▮ (1505)
▭ (1656) Colombo

■▮ (1507) Galle
▭ (1656)

Matara (1507) ■▮
(1656) ▭

ated with a low-caste lifestyle. Another stumbling block was the rampant immorality and corruption among the Portuguese. Apparently, those Portuguese had forgotten or were unaware of the apostle Paul's exhortation to the Colossians to conduct themselves wisely toward outsiders.

In fact, when the Jesuit missionary Frances Xavier landed in India four decades after da Gama, he was convinced that the greatest obstacle to the gospel in India was not the superstitions or Hindu resistance to Christian evangelism. It was the open immorality among the Portuguese. Portuguese men were acquiring slave girls for their harems.

What didn't help matters was Portugal's new agreement with criminals: granting pardon in exchange for living in India permanently. So the combination of greed, immorality, and culturally offensive habits among the Portuguese prevented many Hindus from embracing the gospel. To the Hindu and Muslim in India, all Portuguese were Christians; the two identities were inseparable, so no wonder they were so turned off to the gospel.

As the Jesuits, Franciscans, and other Catholic missionaries arrived from Portugal, they had more than their share of obstacles that were put in place by their homeland. Those clergy who worked solely with the Portuguese in India rather than the indigenous people refused to allow the Franciscans to gather men and women together in the convents to teach them about the Christian faith. Portugal also forbid the missionaries to baptize any Hindu or Muslim slaves that had converted to Christianity, fearing a confrontation with their owners. Indian nationals were not allowed into the priesthood, and most Portuguese refused to learn the languages. This rendered them unable to share the gospel with the indigenous people, contrary to Paul's approach of becoming all things to all people in order to win some to Christ.

Portugal limited their outreach to Indians, refusing to endanger their place in the global trade business for the gospel. Losing it was far too risky. Nonetheless, their lifestyle offended the Indians and they would soon take an action that would cost a Jesuit his life.

In 1549, the Portuguese set up a stockade at a Hindu holy site. The Brahmins objected and found a way to get rid of these foreign blasphemers. The King of Vijayanagara's soldiers (called Badagas) attacked, driving out the Portuguese. Many escaped by sea. But one Jesuit, Antony Criminali, saw women and children left on the shore. As he rushed to help them, he was stabbed in his side. The others jumped on him and tore off his clothes. Managing to get up, he ran toward the church where he had just said mass that morning, and met more assailants. This time he was pierced in his chest, but still he struggled toward the church. Another Badaga stepped in and stabbed him. Criminali fell to his knees. The soldiers showed Criminali no mercy and decapitated him.

Change in Spirit, Change in Tactics
Being charged with coercing conversions didn't help the Portuguese—an accusation some Christians are facing today in India, prompting anti-conversion legislation. (See page 96.) The Portuguese were seeing people convert to Christianity through their hospitals and schools, through visiting prisoners in jail, and requiring Brahmins to attend public lectures in the colonies. The Portuguese also extended privileges to Christians that infuriated Hindus. For example, slaves of Hindus who converted were set free, and widows who converted could claim their inheritance.

The second half of the sixteenth century witnessed a zealotry that didn't help matters for the missionaries. In Portuguese colonies, laws were passed outlawing Hindu rites and criminalizing Hindu idols. Some laws had good results, such as banning the practice of *sati*, or burning a widow along with her deceased husband. But these laws backfired on the missionaries, painting a picture of a demanding God who forced people to worship Him. Such a view exposes a fundamental misunderstanding of the Christian faith as opposed to other creeds. For example, take the apostle Paul's words to the Romans: "Believe on the Lord Jesus Christ and you will be saved." Belief, or faith, cannot be forced. No one can force a person to believe anything. However, if one's "faith" is determined simply by reciting a creed (such as, "There is no god but Allah...."), then one can be forced. Soon the Council of Trent convened, forbidding the missionaries to bring people to Christianity by force, "since no one comes to Christ in faith unless he be drawn by the heavenly Father in freely given love and prevenient [preceding] grace."

With this change in spirit and tactics, the church got the push it needed to further the gospel in India. And as it did, it faced opposition. By the early seventeenth century, the greater part of India was still unaware of Christianity. The country was still steeped in religions, be it Hinduism, Islam, a tribal religion, or some mix. And letters from the Jesuits on the mission field were "full of tales of persecution often valiantly endured."

As the Portuguese established their colonies along India's coast, another front was pushing south, creating more challenges for those who bore the name of Christ—the Mughals of northern India.

INDIA TODAY:
A MASTERPIECE OF FAITH

Their leader was killed and someone had to pay. On August 24, 2008, Hindu extremists attacked Christians in Orissa state, blaming them for his death. The radicals didn't care that a Marxist group had claimed responsibility for the murder. It was an excuse to attack.

Thousands of Christians fled into the neighboring jungle for shelter as the Hindu mob burned homes and beat any who dared remain. One of those men who perished was Monalisha's husband. This is her testimony of faith following the brutal attack that took the life of her husband, a pastor in the village.

My name is Monalisha. [Some were] scattered here and there...121 people dead. There was no food, no water, nothing was there [in the jungle]. Even when we saw the tigers, they were running in jungles but they did not attack us. But these people, they were trying to attack us. We were hiding in the jungle.

I have been living in the camp ever since the 29th of August. Since then, my faith has become stronger. The Word of God has made my faith stronger. The [teachers] used to preach about persecution, how to become strong, to keep a strong faith in God. By listening to all these messages I am becoming very strong. There are preachers in the camps that are talking about persecution, and they're talking about how to be strong in your faith.

I am not afraid, because one day we are going to die. That was God's plan. And my husband was killed, so one day, my children will also. Without God's knowledge nothing will happen, so God [allowed] these things [to] happen...

I am not angry with God for letting this happen. Sometimes I get angry with the Hindus, sometimes I don't get angry. Those who killed my husband would talk to me. They would greet me, saying, "How are you? How are your children? How are you living?"

At first, I was angry, but slowly, slowly, [forgiveness] took a process and now I am not [angry]. I prayed for them. I said, "God, You forgive them and help them to come to You." I also tell my children to pray for them.

Job in the Bible is my hero, because he lost everything and stayed faithful.

I have never thought about turning away from being a Christian and going back to being a Hindu. Whatever happened has happened, so if I die, I'll also die a Christian. I'm not going back.

One day I'll meet [my husband], so the blessing will come when I meet him in heaven.

When my children grow up, I will continue in ministry. I'll walk with Christ. Whatever persecution comes, I'm not going to leave Christ. I'm teaching my children the same thing.

Please tell Christians in America that whatever persecution comes, be strong in Christ so we can overcome.

FACING THE WARRIORS: PERSECUTION UNDER THE MUGHAL EMPIRE (1525-1858)

They were fierce warriors and skilled horsemen, descendants of Genghis Khan who had swept Asia. And they were known to send harsh messages to their enemies: decapitating their victims and displaying their heads. Now these Mongols, or Mughals as the Indians referred to them, looked to conquer and control the great riches of India.

Already dominated by Muslims, the sultanates of northern India were unprepared for the advanced weaponry of the Mughals, commanded by Babur. Composite bows penetrated armor, and cannons with a range of more than a thousand yards brought a crushing defeat on Ibrahim Lodhi's men in Delhi in 1525.

Thus began the Mughal Empire, which lasted more than three hundred years. And at the hands of their new rulers, Christians would face times of both freedom and persecution with moments of glory.

Hopes for Another Constantine

The Christian merchants were caught. The Jesuits in the area learned that the businessmen had failed to pay their taxes to the emperor, and the Jesuits called them on it. Akbar—the Mughal's third emperor—took notice.

Having already abolished the hated *jizya*, or poll tax, on all non-Muslims and created marriage alliances with the local wealthy Hindu landowners called *Rajputs*, Akbar seized the opportunity to expand his knowledge to yet another group—the Jesuits. In 1575, he had built the *Ibadat Khana* ("hall of worship" or more accurately described as the "debating hall"), where every Thursday he debated with Hindus, Muslims, Parsees,[7] and followers of other religions. Now he had another religion to bring into the weekly symposium by inviting the Jesuits.

Knowing they could run the risk of martyrdom, the Jesuits went anyway, seeing their chance to convert Akbar to Christianity. They hoped he would be another Constantine and bring Islam to an end in the region, as the legendary emperor had ended idol worship in the Roman Empire. They even gave Akbar a copy of *The Polyglot of the Bible*—six volumes of the Bible in several different languages. It is said that Akbar wanted to know which volume contained the *injil* (Gospels) and later expressed a great respect for this volume. The Jesuits were hopeful.

But the debates were going nowhere. One of the Jesuits wrote that he was deeply distressed during one of the debates. When he had said, "Christ Jesus, Son of God," one of the Muslims

---

7 Parsees are descendents of followers of the Zoroastrian religion believed to have fled Persia to northern India when Islam invaded during the seventh century.

Akbar's inter-faith dialogue. The two
Jesuits in attendance are in the dark robes.

cried out, *"Astafarla!"* ("God forbid!") Another covered his ears, and a third mocked.

It was no surprise that Akbar's tolerance was not shared by all Muslim citizens in his empire. The Christians in Lahore (now in present-day Pakistan) were being mistreated, and the Jesuits used their influence to convince Akbar to issue a royal command in writing that all could freely become Christians without any interference. Muslim officers in Lahore tried to hinder the issuance of these letters, but in 1602 Akbar insisted on their proclamation.

Still, some Muslims found ways to defy his orders and mistreated Christians in Lahore and Agra, the new capital of the Mughal Empire. One source says that during Akbar's reign, Muslims who opposed his hand of tolerance rebelled, causing the Jesuits' favor to diminish slightly, but the Jesuits still found ways to preach and lead others to Christ.

In time, the Jesuits' hopes for a Mughal version of Constantine faded. Calling a General Council and inviting all scholars and military commanders of the cities, Akbar announced his newly created religion called *Din-i-Ilahi* ("the divine faith"), with Akbar as a somewhat divine figure. Apparently his intent was to create "one perfect and universal religion."

Akbar had no intention of becoming a Christian. When he died in 1605, his religion died with him.

A New Emperor

Despite the Jesuits' disappointment, they continued occasional public discussions. One Muslim who was particularly kind toward the Jesuits heard them speak of the many vices and crimes committed by the Prophet Mohammed. He advised them, very likely with a high degree of emotion, to speak about Islam carefully, admitting that he "boiled with indignation and felt himself inclined to stab them with his dagger" when he heard their arguments against Islam's prophet.[8]

One of the Jesuits, Jerome Xavier, later concluded that religious discussion that turned to "violent controversy" wasn't the right method for sharing about Christ. He wrote: "The sword is not a key giving admission to the heart, never, never. It is reasons, instruction, good example, tenderness and benefits that open well-locked hearts. That key was used by Jesus Christ, our Lord, whereas Mohammed wielded the sword."[9]

Now with Akbar dead, the Jesuits looked to his son, the Prince Salim, with hopes that he would extend the same favor toward the Jesuits' preaching and evangelism. He didn't. In fact, what secured Salim's succession to the throne was a promise to restore the law of Mohammed to its previous honor. He ordered the mosques to

8 Neill, p. 182.

9 Ibid., p. 183.

be cleaned and Muslim fasts restored. And as emperor, he took new titles, one of which was *Jahangir*, meaning "conqueror of the world." And what he did next raised the Jesuits' suspicions that their freedom to preach might be fleeting.

Salim called for two sons of an Armenian to be brought before him. He ordered them to convert to Islam, but the youth refused. Exerting his power, he ordered his men to circumcise the boys... right in front of him.

Hoping he had proved a point, Salim told the boys to recite the Muslim profession of faith. Again, they wouldn't. Indignant, Salim had them flogged until finally, they gave in.

Their bodies bruised and aching, the young boys were distraught. When the Jesuits saw them, one of the boys cried, "I am a Christian! I am a Christian!" and through tears said his profession of Muslim faith was given only because of the pain they endured.

Then according to one source, that was the end of Salim's outward hostility toward Christians and he exhibited a more friendly face toward them.

Surprisingly, three years after the incident, Salim requested that the Jesuits instruct and baptize three of his nephews. While it appeared to be an open door for the Jesuits to convert the entire ruling family, the desired result didn't happen. Many questioned Salim's motives for having the boys instructed, speculating that it could have been a ploy to disqualify them from the throne or introduce them to Portuguese women and take them as brides to further political alliances. The mystery remains, and the gospel didn't penetrate the heart of this Mughal emperor whose sworn loyalties to Islam secured his place on the throne.

Still, the Jesuits kept seeking converts among the higher ranks of society as new emperors would ascend and oppose their efforts. At this time in history, the church in Rome still viewed the throne and the church as one. The separation of church and state was a foreign, if not, heretical concept, and the Body of Christ was not viewed as independent of secular rulers. This mentality became more of a liability than a legality and would cost the church precious time in gospel-preaching and disciple-making.

Shah Jahan

He built what some consider one of the greatest, most beautiful buildings in the world—the Taj Mahal. Shah Jahan took the throne but did not look kindly on the Christians. He would soon demolish churches and wage a war against the Portuguese, whom he equated with Christianity.

Having set up a base in Hugli, the lower valley of the Ganges River, the Portuguese indulged in behavior that Shah Jahan despised. In fact, one source rightfully refers to their behavior as "abominable." The Portuguese imposed a high customs duty on salt, kidnapped Bengali children to sell them as slaves, and engaged in piracy. The priests heard of the emperor's impending threat and alerted the Portuguese, but they ignored the Jesuits' warnings.

Finally, in 1632, Shah Jahan had had enough and ordered an attack. Many Portuguese were captured and taken to Agra. One source claims more than four thousand Christians were made prisoners and taken to Agra before Shah Jahan

Shah Jahan

and offered the "choice between conversion to Islam and confinement or slavery under abjectly severe conditions."[10] Another source says only four hundred survived the eleven-month journey. Four priests who survived were whipped, paraded through town, and imprisoned. Two clergy died in prison. After the attack, Muslims tried to convert the Christians to Islam. Many women and children complied, while others refused. Some were released. An anti-Christian edict was issued, apparently forbidding the construction of any new churches.

---

10 Edwardes and Garrett, p. 75.

Shah Jahan also hindered the spread of Hinduism. He prohibited Muslims from converting to Hinduism, wouldn't permit Hindus to build new temples, and had those in the process of construction torn down.

Years later, Shah Jahan rescinded his ban on new church buildings, but still didn't allow the construction of Hindu temples and razed those begun.

The Last of the Mughals
In the final decades of the Mughal Empire, it was much of the same: edicts against non-Muslims and occasional outright persecution against Christians. The *jizya* was reinstated under Aurungzeb, unearthing resentment among non-Muslims required to pay the high tax.

Still struggling to penetrate the Muslim north with the gospel, the Jesuits kept focusing on the conversion of higher social classes and imperial officials while others were taking the gospel to southern India, in places where neither Portuguese nor Muslims ruled. And many would suffer for turning to Christ, causing the tale of glory to continue.

STORY FROM HISTORY:
A BRAHMIN TAUNTED FOR CHRIST

Hundreds flocked to the streets as they followed the roar of the crowd. Shops were closed and work was abandoned. They had to see this young man named Polada who dared to abandon his religion and his high-caste status as a Brahmin for the God of the Jesuits.

Polada walked through the streets as insults were hurled his way.

"How dare you shame your family!"

"You are a Brahmin, not a worthless Christian!"

Polada bravely pushed through the crowd on his way to court. "You speak these things," he responded, "because you do not know what you are saying." Never before had he experienced such peace—and, of all places, in the midst of a hate-filled mob. This was seventeenth-century Mughal India.

Some managed to strike or kick Polada as he walked by. But almost all had the same look—a mixture of horror and shame and shock.

Finally, Polada reached the judge.

"You have brought your parents much sorrow for embracing this worthless law," the judge said sternly to the young man. "I have collected almost enough rupees so you can go and cleanse yourself in the Ganges River and rid yourself of this Christianity![11] This money will give you a very comfortable life."

Unflinching, the young man replied, "For the torments of hell, and the loss of my soul, both of which I should suffer by following your advice, your two thousand rupees would comfort me no better than this spittle."

With those words, he spit on the ground and told the judge that he would rather have a worthless coin and live on the lowest doorstep with the Jesuits than accept his money.

"You deserve death if you don't abandon this Christian nonsense!" yelled the judge at the young convert.

"Do your will!" Polada replied. "I am quite ready to die; for it has long been my greatest desire. It is a very strange thing that when any Gentile wishes to become a [Hindu] or a Muslim, no one stands in his way; but when he wishes to become a Christian, it seems that the Devil and hell are leagued against him, to turn him from his purpose."

When Polada finished speaking, the judge turned to his parents. "Your child is lost. He is not worth any further trouble."

The judge sent Polada back into the streets where the abuse he faced from the crowd intensified. But his trouble was not yet over. A Muslim

---

11 Hindus believed that washing in the Ganges River cleansed a person from his sins.

leader ordered that he forfeit all his belongings and anything he would inherit. Then he was handed over to the Jesuits, who instructed this courageous young man in the faith. But his example had already instructed them!

FACING THE RAJAHS:
PERSECUTION IN SOUTH INDIA
(16TH–18TH CENTURIES)

The Muslim Mughals ruled most of India. The Portuguese were claiming territory along parts of India's coast. And outside the realm of the Portuguese colonies, pockets of independent Indian territories remained ruled by rajahs, Indian kings, and princes.

As additional missionaries arrived from Portugal, some were fed up with their predecessors' overindulgent lifestyles that hindered the gospel. The city of Goa was already saturated with priests, so some set their sights outside the colonies. One of these missionaries was Francis Xavier who arrived in India in 1542.

When offered the chance to minister outside the colonies, Xavier accepted without hesitation. He traveled south to the village of Cape Comorin on the Fisher Coast to work with the Paravas, a lower caste people. Many Paravas had already come to Christ several years earlier but only because they saw the Portuguese as their protectors against the raiding Muslim fleets. Thus, they were "Christians" in name only, not in practice or conviction.

In time, Xavier led many to genuine conversion, yet others were afraid to take that step. Frustrated, Xavier was convinced the Brahmins were the cause. Brahmins deceived the lower castes, saying that if the Paravas didn't bring an offering to the gods, the gods would cause them to get sick or die or possibly even send demons to their houses. Still, he lived among them and patiently shared the gospel. In other colonies, Christians were subjected to Indian rulers who were more erratic, impulsive, and unpredictable toward them than toward their Muslim neighbors.

Some say the persecution of Christians was isolated and infrequent, rather than systematic or government-instigated. There were exceptions, such as the martyrdom of John de Britto, who was executed for his faith by an Indian king. It was the price he paid for seeing such an encouraging response to the gospel among all Hindu castes.

Born of Portuguese nobility, de Britto could have aspired to almost any prestigious career, but he chose instead to join the Jesuits and take the gospel to India. He set sail for India, and his voyage was the first of many challenges that would serve to confirm and deepen his resolve to evangelize, rather than head back to a mother who had tried to persuade a church leader not to let him go.

An epidemic broke out on the ship, infecting one of his Jesuit companions, but he evaded it and landed in Goa in 1673. From Goa, he journeyed to Kerala and then through the mountains to the Madurai mission. There he faced another challenge, this time from nature, and endured a flood.

Having a disregard for danger, de Britto was undeterred and saw many come to Christ.

But de Britto's success in leading people to Christ did not go unnoticed. A group of Brahmins were furious with him. That he was a skilled debater and Brahmins rarely won an argument was perhaps another reason they needed to stop him. Soon they found a way.

In July 1686, de Britto was arrested along with two catechists[12] and three other Christians. For fifteen days they were tortured. All but one endured.

Amazed at the men's resilient faith, the king of Marava released them but with one condition: they couldn't share their "strange doctrines."

De Britto returned to Portugal in 1688, but couldn't stay away from India. He returned to the subcontinent in November 1689 and headed straight for Marava.

The ruler might have overlooked de Britto's presence in his kingdom, but de Britto converted one of the king's relatives. When this relative turned to Christ, he decided to put away his secondary wives—one of whom was the king's niece.

The king could ignore the missionary no longer: de Britto needed to die, as he was the one

---

12 A catechist is one who instructs another in religious matters, especially church doctrine.

who brought shame on the king's family. The king had him arrested and tried to have him killed using magic and sorcery, but those attempts failed.

As de Britto sat in prison awaiting his death, he wrote letters that were smuggled out to fellow Jesuits, telling them: "I am at present in prison, awaiting the death which I am about to suffer for my God. It was the hope of attaining this happiness which constrained me a second time to visit India."

On February 4, 1693, he was beheaded with a scimitar (curved sword).

As persecution continued to occur sporadically in parts of India, missionaries were finding further challenges to the gospel. For example, Robert Nobili found the Hindu teaching of karma the greatest obstacle for evangelism, as Indian nationals couldn't accept that they were created with a free will. He was one of several who had taken the apostle Paul's teaching of becoming "all things to all men, that I might by all means save some" (1 Corinthians 9:22).

In the 1700s, a different kind of Christian would arrive—the Protestants—creating a fresh approach to outreach on the subcontinent. But their journey to India wouldn't come without hindrance by an unlikely foe.

WORDS OF GLORY FROM TODAY'S PERSECUTED CHURCH

"I never imagined that they would kill him [my husband]....God will never do injustice. This is His will for my life. There can be no greater happiness and blessing than to know my husband died a martyr for Christ."

—HEPSEBAH, whose husband was killed
by radical Hindus around 2004

"I believe God will transform my problems into a program for His glory."

—RANJAN KUMAR DANGUA, captured
and beaten in 2005 by Hindu radicals
trying to force him to deny Christ

"We tell our persecution story not so anyone will pity us, but so that people will see our victory in Christ. Our persecution is a story of victory!"

—PAUL, who with his wife had everything they
owned stolen by a Hindu mob around 2008

"I am a strong believer in Jesus Christ. You may kill me but I will never become Hindu."

—PASTOR KANTHESWAR DIGAL, who was killed by Hindu radicals in September 2008, on returning to his home in Orissa after his family was forced to flee in an August attack

"I am greatly upset but not angry."

—GLADYS STAINES in a phone interview after her husband and two sons were murdered in Orissa in January 1999

POWER OVER PROCLAMATION: THE PROTESTANT ARRIVAL (18TH CENTURY)

The Dutch and French had arrived in the wake of Portuguese traders. Now the British had decided it was their turn to capitalize on India's great wealth, but there was one problem: missionaries.

Christians from England and America felt compelled to take the gospel to the land of the Hindus. Many were convinced that the gospel alone held the power to break the chains of thousands of years of caste discrimination and poverty.

But the British East India Company (BEIC) didn't care. They didn't want anything or anyone hindering their potential earnings or position in Britain's crown jewel called India. And it wouldn't be until the early 1800s that the BEIC's charter would be challenged and changed to allow licenses to missionaries to reside in India.

* * *

An Unlikely Foe
Although the BEIC appointed chaplains, they were only to minister to the merchants and military. At times they were allowed to help the Indians through acts of service, but outright gospel proclamation was prohibited for fear of offending the non-Christian population. The evangelical community was rightfully outraged, as shown in

the words of Baptist minister Robert Hall: "For a Christian nation to give decided preference to polytheism and idolatry by prohibiting the dissemination of a purer faith, and thus employ its powers in suppressing the truth...is repugnant ....We have no example in the history of the world of such a conduct; we have no precedent of a people prohibiting the propagation of their own faith."[13]

By the end of the 1700s, BEIC policies turned openly anti-missionary. Any Briton wishing to go to India was required to obtain a license from the BEIC, and captains of BEIC ships sailing for India caught carrying any unlicensed people, specifically missionaries, risked losing their appointment and possibly even ruining their life. One captain created a stir when he took an interest in a young Bengali who asked to be baptized. The BEIC became alarmed and told the captain he needed approval from England. Almost two years later, the captain finally secured permission for the young boy to be baptized.

A Detriment to the Danes

Open hostility toward missionaries was not exclusive to Britain and her colonies in India. A Danish colony gave two German Pietists[14] named Bartholamaeus Ziegenbalg and Heinrich Plutschaw

---

13 Moffett, pp. 263–264.

14 A Pietist is one who follows Pietism, a movement within Lutheranism that stressed personal piety.

an unfriendly welcome. Unfazed by the cool reception, they learned Tamil, the language of the Indians in the colony, and preached the gospel to them, seeing many come to Christ. They even built churches. But the governor did not like the German missionaries' work. In an unpublished man-

Ziegenbalg, missionary to India

uscript, Ziegenbalg wrote, "The more we spoke the truth the more were we persecuted, so that at last it seemed as if they wished to exterminate both us and our congregations."[15]

Eventually the Danish governor lashed out and threw Ziegenbalg in jail. Apparently, Ziegenbalg had stepped over the line when he intervened on behalf of a widow who asked for his assistance. During four months of solitary confinement, the missionary encouraged himself with hymns and prayer. At one point during his imprisonment, he fell on his knees and prayed with such fervor that it made a great impression on his guards.

---

15 Fenger and Fancke, p. 39.

Finally he was released, but the imprisonment didn't deter Ziegenbalg. As he preached in
the church, crowds of Indians crammed into the
building to hear what he had to say.

Soon Ziegenbalg felt compelled to preach in
India's interior and left the Danish colony. His
friends warned him that the king in that area did
not allow white men, but they were wrong. The
king warmly welcomed him, unlike the reception
he received from the Danes.

This was not the case in every independently
controlled kingdom scattered throughout the
country. In the area of Tranquebar, Europeans
were confined to their coastal colonies and were
not welcome in the surrounding kingdoms. Missionaries were still able to get the gospel into
these forbidden areas, however, as Indian converts
were allowed to move freely across the borders
into Indian territory. Still, the BEIC put up a fight
to keep British missionaries off the subcontinent.

Kicked Out of the Colony
Despite the anti-missionary policies of the BEIC,
missionaries found ways to the subcontinent.
One enterprising missionary was a young Baptist
named William Carey.

When Carey announced his plans to go to
India, his father thought that he had lost his
mind, and his wife refused to go unless her sister
accompanied her. An elder in the church even

told Carey that if God was interested in saving the heathen, He'd find a way to do it Himself.

Undeterred, Carey and his family left for India in June 1793. Somehow they had managed to board a BEIC ship. But once the ship had set sail and the captain was informed of William's reasons for going to India, he and his family were ordered to disembark as soon as they reached the Channel. Managing to obtain passage on a Dutch vessel, they continued their five-month voyage to the subcontinent.

When the Careys stepped foot in Calcutta months after they departed their native England, they were not welcomed at all. The British colonial government was still refusing to grant residence permits to missionaries, so they were forced to leave. Almost penniless and without a home, they finally found refuge in a Catholic Portuguese settlement. Only when a group of indigo planters took pity on the poor missionary did he have employment, allowing him and his family to live in British territory.

William Carey

More missionaries arrived to join the Careys in their work. Eventually the Baptist group moved upriver to the Danish colony of Serampore where they organized themselves into a voluntary, self-supporting mission.

It wasn't until 1800 that Carey baptized his first convert. Then in 1802, a Brahmin came to Christ, giving up his friends and his caste. Added to Carey's challenges to preach Christ on the subcontinent, his wife's mental health quickly deteriorated.

As William Carey and the Serampore mission were seeing Indians come to Christ, the BEIC continued thwarting the arrival of more missionaries. Critics of the BEIC said a man with a Bible was considered "doubly dangerous." And once missionaries stepped foot on the subcontinent, they were hard to get rid of, so the BEIC did what it could, even preventing their departure to India.

Robert Haldane, a wealthy Scot, was one BEIC "success story." In 1796, he organized the founding of a mission in India. He was prepared to sell his estate, invest £25,000 to support the ongoing work, and even go as one of the missionaries. He had a team of teachers and a printing press ready to go, but the BEIC refused to grant him a license to set up the mission anywhere in its territory. One of the BEIC's directors even went so far as saying that he would prefer seeing a "band of devils in India than a band of missionaries."[16]

Then there's the London Missionary Society, which sent out its first missionary to India in

16 Smith, p. 170.

1798. But once he arrived in Calcutta, the British expatriates made him feel so unwelcome that he moved to a neighboring European settlement, much like Carey's Serampore Baptists.

"Imprudent" and "Injudicious"

The British felt justified in their actions against the missionaries. Protecting their business interests in their new crown jewel was a high priority and any instability among their native employees could be disastrous, they claimed. Soon, the BEIC would allege that the Vellore Mutiny of 1807 was the result of zealous attempts—or rumored attempts—to convert the Indians.[17]

Sir John Craddock, the commander-in-chief of the Madras Army, issued new orders to all ranks of the sepoys. (Sepoys were native Indians employed by the British to protect colonial interests, essentially a private infantry for the BEIC.) Displeased with the "military smartness of the troops on parade," he introduced a new turban and required that caste marks not be visible. The sepoys also had to have a clean-shaven chin and a uniform moustache.

To the sepoys, the new requirements were unacceptable. The new turban looked like the caps worn by the regimented drummers, members of a despised caste. So in July 1807, they revolted, killing almost one hundred British.

---

17 Vellore is located about a hundred miles west of Madras.

In addition, a rumor was circulating blaming the zeal of Christian missionaries for implanting the notion that Sir Craddock's changes were ultimately intended to convert them to Christianity. Where that rumor started is unknown. Some say a single sentence in the commander-in-chief's report suggested that the sepoys may have thought the next step was conversion to Christianity. But there was no documentation of the source of such an idea.

A year after the Vellore Mutiny, the BEIC Court of Directors dispatched these words: "We are very far from being averse to the introduction of Christianity into India...but nothing could be more unwise than any imprudent or injudicious attempt to induce it by means which should irritate and alarm their religious prejudices...." But the intention of not opposing Christian missions was overshadowed when the dispatch continued: "The paramount power which we now possess in India...imposes upon us the necessity... to protect the native inhabitants in the free and undisturbed profession of their religious opinions, and to take care that they are neither harassed nor irritated by any premature or over-zealous attempts to convert them to Christianity."[18]

The BEIC's policy of thwarting the efforts of any incoming missionaries remained.

---

18 Philips, p. 164.

Fives years after the Vellore Mutiny, two missionaries with the American Missionary Board, Adonirum Judson and Samuel Newell, arrived in Calcutta. The police were notified, and the public was made aware that the two Americans had come to establish a mission in Bengal. They were immediately deported.

A few weeks after Judson and Newell were kicked out of India, six more missionaries arrived —three from England and three from America. In the words of one writer, "At such an abundance [of missionaries] the anxious English were filled with terror."[19] Several were shipped back where the BEIC required reimbursement for their return voyage. However, two of the Americans escaped to Bombay, where a letter of arrest was sent after them, ordering their departure to England.

The Charter's Change

Every twenty years the BEIC was required to submit its charter to Parliament for review and renewal. The BEIC faced a flurry of public criticism for its anti-missionary policies. The rise of English evangelicalism in the wake of the Wesleyan revivals fueled the drive to confront the BEIC's outright actions against missionaries.

With the help of William Wilberforce, who had just won the battle outlawing slavery, a new charter was issued in 1813, ordering the creation

---

19 Richter, p. 144.

of an Anglican church in India. But most importantly, it granted missionaries residence and the freedom to preach.

Even though this new "edict of toleration" had authority only in British-controlled areas in India, the missionaries saw the opportunity and pushed through. And as they came, they faced opposition from both fellow Christians and native Indians. One of these missionaries was Alexander Duff.

Duff reached out to India's Brahmins. His unconventional approach to missions soon caught the attention of fellow missionaries. In fact, some say fellow missionaries were as critical of his efforts as the militant Hindus. What was so objectionable about his outreach methods? He taught English to Hindus, as well as Bible and Western studies like economics. Duff did have a few fans, one of whom was the aging William Carey.

As missionaries questioned Duff's tactics, Hindu opposition grew. When rumors spread that Duff was defiling his Hindu upper-caste students by placing a Bible in their hands and asking them to read it, the weekly Bible lectures he held in his home quickly dwindled from three hundred to five students. But when three of the Hindu students asked for baptism, the Hindus were incensed. One of the students, Gopinath Nandi, who would later found an orphanage at Futtehgurh, was kicked out of his family.

As the Protestants preached to nonbelievers, the ancient church that links its origins to the apostle Thomas continued. One English mission to Kerala, where a great number of Thomas Christians had settled, was given the instruction not to remove the ancient church and start another but to restore the places where they were dying spiritually.

Around the mid-nineteenth century, mass movements of outcastes—the Dalits, or untouchables—were coming to Christ. Their witness was contagious. Some Christian historians believe this wave of conversions in the last part of the nineteenth century was pivotal for Christianity in India. And it was a shift that would be felt well into the twentieth century, causing a surge in Indian nationalism that would fuel independence and future opposition.

STORY FROM HISTORY:
A RAJAH LOSES
ALL FOR CHRIST

He had nothing to gain and everything to lose. U Borsing was heir to the throne of his kingdom in the remote Khasi Hills of northeast India. People already referred to him as their ruler, their "Rajah." Now with missionaries in his region, he was confronted with a new kingdom—the kingdom of Jesus Christ—and faced a choice that would cost him everything he possessed.

Before the arrival of the Welsh missionaries, Borsing had never heard of Jesus. Many of those in his village who had left their tribal religion for Christianity suffered greatly, like one young girl named Ka Chot whose decision infuriated her family.

One night Ka Chot's mother and one of her older sisters visited her at the missionary's station. Having already suffered at the hands of her family, Ka was surprised that her mother and sister were so affectionate and kind to her. Suddenly, her mother threw herself to the floor and claimed to be ill. The other women at the station ran to Ka's mother to see if she was okay. Having duped the women into believing she was truly sick, Ka's mother strained to get to her feet and asked Ka to help her part of the way home.

Ka wasn't sure. She knew her mother's past hostility toward her and hesitated.

"Have pity on your poor mother," the other women told her.

Ka gave in to the persuasive words and left with her mother and sister.

One of the village converts saw Ka Chot leave. Knowing her family's history of cruelty, he decided to follow them at a distance.

After a walking a while, Ka told her mother it was time for her to return to the mission station. Just then, her "feeble" mother straightened up, grabbed Ka, ripped off her clothes and beat her. The young man who had followed them tried to pull Ka's mother off of her, but the mother turned on him and struck him with a blow and kick that sent him running. Somehow, Ka managed to escape and returned to the mission station bruised, bleeding, and naked.

Borsing had heard about Ka's case and knew what happened to those who left their village religion. So did his wife. It was no secret that his wife hated the missionaries. However, when their oldest son became very sick, that all changed.

As the son's condition worsened, he told his mother that the missionaries' teaching had convinced him to leave his religion and turn to Christ. His mother cried out to the demons every day, begging them to heal him. But they didn't.

He died. Instead of becoming further embittered toward the missionaries, her faith in the demons was shattered, and she and six of her daughters turned to Christ.

Five months later, Borsing and the rest of his children placed their faith in Christ. Word spread of the future rajah turning his back on his religion and accepting the religion of the foreign missionaries. If he ascended the throne, Borsing would also be expected to be the religious head of his village. Now as a Christian, he knew he would be forced to make a choice.

No more than six months later, that day came.

The reigning rajah died, and Borsing was the next in line to the throne.

The chiefs asked him to turn back to Hinduism, but he refused. "I can throw off my cloak or my turban," he told them, "but the covenant I have made with God I can no wise cast away."

Borsing's nephew stepped up and claimed the throne. Soon after his nephew became the rajah of Cherra, he confiscated all of Borsing's belongings and means of support. Borsing was now left with nothing—all because he turned to Christ.

In a letter, Borsing wrote to one of the missionaries: "Whether I gain or lose, it will not make any difference with regard to me. The Lord's will be done. If I am stripped naked, what difference will it make? I have the Lord Jesus as my portion."

STARING DOWN DEATH:
THE GREAT MUTINY (1857)

British troops were dangerously outnumbered. With twenty sepoys to every one British soldier, the foreigners wouldn't stand a chance if the Indian nationals turned on them. And that's exactly what happened . . . and it all began with a rumor.

The British introduced new rifle cartridges, requiring the sepoys to bite them off before loading their weapon. "The cartridges are spread with cow and pig fat!" flew the rumor.

Consisting of both Hindus and Muslims, the sepoys were furious at their foreign superiors. To the Muslim, a pig was an abomination. To the Hindu, the cow was sacred.

The rumor quickly fueled a riot.

Refusing to leave their religion undefended, the sepoy army in Bengal rebelled, seizing the city of Delhi, massacring every European they found.[20] They even dragged the last Mughal emperor, Bahadur Shah III, out of retirement and installed him as their leader.

What was to be called the "Mutiny" began to spread across north and central India, and with it came blood-letting violence and cold-hearted destruction. In Kanpur, women and children were

---

20 The sepoys were centered in Bombay, Madras, and Bengal. Only those in Bengal rebelled during the Mutiny. The others remained loyal to the British.

butchered in cold blood, and cities were destroyed in the army's path.

Missionaries were not exempt from the bloodshed. And the story of those from the Futtehgurh mission station is one that is nothing less than glorious.

The Mission and the "Infidel Dogs"

Situated on the west side of the Ganges River in north central India, the picturesque Christian village of Futtehgurh had sprung up almost twenty years earlier when Reverend Gopinath Nandi, a convert of Alexander Duff's ministry, started an orphanage. A famine had hit the surrounding area, lining the roads for miles with beggars and abandoned or orphaned children. In time, the orphanage was surrounded by thatched houses and flat-roofed buildings. A school was even built.

The Sepoy Mutiny

Missionaries from America came to work alongside the Indian nationals. They preached in bazaars and villages, and in time their small congregation grew. Even an Indian rajah turned to Christ and donated funds to their new church building.

During the spring of 1857, reports of the Great Mutiny in Meerut and Delhi reached the Futtehgurh missionaries, sparing no detail as to the brutalities the sepoys invoked on any Westerner. Soon, they heard that the sepoys were approaching their mission.

Deeply anguished, the missionaries prayed for wisdom. The suspense was unsettling. They knew they could face certain death when the sepoys reached their mission, unless a miraculous change in events took place. However, they didn't want to leave behind the nationals who had come to Christ. The missionaries were sure these converts would also die in the carnage. The Muslims who had turned to Christ were already being taunted in the nearby city. "Where is your Jesus now?" taunted the Muslims. "We will shortly show what will become of the infidel dogs."

As the missionaries prayed and waited on the Lord for wisdom, they took precautions. Every night the men patrolled the village and kept their horses ready should they need a quick escape.

Soon word came of a massacre in Shahjahanpore. Reverend J. McCallum and his congregation were slain in the church. Only one managed to escape to tell the fate of his fellow worshipers. When the missionaries heard, they decided it was time to prepare the boats to leave for Cawnpore. But the missionaries had more to prepare than just boats. They needed to prepare the nationals for the inevitable.

One of the missionaries, David Campbell, walked the garden at the mission station with several of the nationals, encouraging them to stand strong in Christ. "We have little hope of escaping," he told them. He felt less concern for himself than for them.

Just then a believer named Ishwuree Dass told him, "The Lord reigneth."

"That is true," replied Campbell, "but blood may be shed."

The time finally came, and the Futtehgurh missionaries boarded their boats and headed down the Ganges River.

It wasn't long before the white-faced gospel messengers were fired upon by hostile villagers and sepoy rebels along the shore. After escaping another firestorm of bullets, the group decided it was best to stay together, so they moved onto one of the boats and loaded their luggage on the other.

Famished and needing nourishment, they sailed their boats to shore, all the while a landholder and his men surrounded the missionaries.

"We don't want blood," he told the missionaries. "We want money."

After the missionaries paid the landholder $500, he promised to guard them. The landholder and some of his men boarded the boats and continued down the river.

For two days and two nights, they sailed without stopping, until their boat struck an island and once again they were surrounded, this time by hostile sepoys.

The missionaries managed to flee from the boats and hid in the long grass on the island. Knowing their capture was imminent, they comforted each other by singing hymns. One of the missionaries, John Freeman, prayed. Then David Campbell spoke of the riches of God's grace. Another prayed.

Finally, the sepoys honed in on their prey, and the missionaries were captured, tied together with rope, and led away. But not all the missionaries had given up on escape. Mr. McLean offered the captors money, hoping they would take the bait as the landholder had.

Rev. John Edgar Freeman

"It is blood we want, not money," one sepoy replied.

As the sepoys led the missionaries and their families away, those they passed jeered at them until finally they were led to their death and shot.

The mission at Futtehgurh was ransacked and destroyed. Many of the Indian nationals faced grave suffering or death.

Reverend Nandi, who founded the orphanage, and his wife and three children were forced to flee. They wandered, not knowing where they were going. Fatigued and hungry, they were robbed of their clothes and their Bible. Another time they were beaten and imprisoned. More than once they were threatened with death if they refused to deny Christ.

The wife of John Houston, a native convert through the orphanage ministry, somehow separated from their group when they fled. She and their infant child were found dead in a hut at the edge of a village. The Muslims wouldn't help her because she and her child weren't Muslim, and the Hindus feared losing caste if they assisted them.

Words of Glory
But the glory of this tale does not lie in the drama of their death or the adventure in their escape. It is found in the depths of their hearts as they stared death in the face and with their final words gave the glory to God.

As the missionaries received word of the impending attack, several wrote letters. They knew death was more probable than life. But their words were not laced with fear and anxiety. They fully rested on the One whose plan and purpose were far better than theirs.

In a letter to her sister, Elizabeth Freeman shared, "I sometimes think our deaths would do more good than we would in all our lives; if

Mrs. Elizabeth Freeman

so, 'His will be done.' Should I be called to lay down my life, do not be grieved, dear sister, that I am here, for most joyfully will I die for him who laid down his life for me."

David Campbell wrote to a fellow missionary, "The Savior is doing something I know to hasten his kingdom, otherwise the Devil would not be in such a tumult about the stability of his."

Amanda Johnson wrote to her sister, "If it be the will of a gracious God that we fall by their hands, oh! that it may be a happy transition to be with Jesus! Our only hope is in Him, and He will not disappoint us."

Her husband, Albert, penned, "Although trials and sorrows may avail us in this dark land, and we be called upon to part with life for Christ and His cause, may we not glorify Him more by our death than by our life?"

After the mutiny, Reverend Fullerton visited Futtehgurh and found two Indian national converts who had fled in the attack—a blind boy named Lullu and a leper named Khurga. They wandered for days, many without shelter. When Fullerton found the two living in a shed, Lullu was sick with a fever.

Fullerton asked Lullu, "Did you find Christ precious during the long months of suffering?"

"Oh, yes! In *dukh* [pain] and in *sukh* [joy], He is ever the same," replied Lullu.

But the tale didn't end here. News of the martyred missionaries reached the ears of Westerners. Any who thought the unsaved Indians were not morally depraved and that their sincerity would be accounted sufficient for entry into heaven were proved wrong. The blood cruelly shed in the Mutiny proved that India—like the rest of the world—indeed needed to hear about the Savior, Jesus Christ.

In the decades to come, Hindu nationalism would begin to take root in the heart of India, transitioning the religion from a superstition into a social force that would continue to persecute God's people.

WORDS OF GLORY
FROM HISTORY

"I am in God's hand: if it is His will that I should be King, I shall be; but if it is not His will, what use is it to struggle against God's great Providence? As a Khasi, I do not desire to be; if the people will take me as I am— that is all."

—U BORSING, heir to the throne as rajah of Cherra, on what he would do if asked to ascend the throne which would require him to return to Hinduism, circa 1875 (Read U Borsing's story on page 74.)

"It is a very little matter for me to lay down my poor life for One so good as Jesus ... Besides that ... it is impossible for them to kill my soul; ... and therefore, what I now feel by grace, they can neither destroy nor take away. And if you were all to run away, and go back to England ...; I feel I can never forget God's word; and if I were left here alone ..., I would still try to cleave to the Lord."

—A YOUNG MAN, asked if he feared the consequences of becoming a Christian, circa 1845

"Pray not only for my sinful soul, that I may be kept faithful unto death, but also, and especially, for the souls of the poor heathens around me, that they may soon be freed from the chains of Satan and be blessed in the name of Jesus. Whether I live or die, let Christ be glorified by the ingathering of sinners to Him. I have many more trials and temptations yet to meet, but oh, may I cut short all of them through Him who is ever gracious to me...."

—REV. GOPINATH NANDI, a Brahmin convert to Christ, in a letter to Alexander Duff, circa 1835

UPSETTING THE SOCIAL ORDER: RISE OF HINDUTVA (19ᵀᴴ-21ˢᵀ CENTURIES)

The people had been ruled by foreign powers for centuries: first the Turks, then the Mughals, now Western businessmen bent on making a profit off the subcontinent's rich resources. The Mughal emperor Aurungzehad had oppressed the Hindus, and some of the Portuguese at times did the same. Now the missionaries were causing the Dalits and others to break from their low-caste status, upsetting the Hindu social order.

Hindus had had enough, and they were ready for change. But it had to be on their terms. Change would come in the form of a Hindu renaissance —and from an unlikely source and later transform into an ugly and fierce social force in the name of a purely Hindu nation that would lash out at Christians.

* * *

The British soon unearthed more than India's wealth of spices, silk, and precious jewels. During the eighteenth century, scholars began digging up the subcontinent's ancient past, discovering and injecting a rebirth in the Hindu religion and culture. Sanskrit classics were being translated into English, influencing Europe's writers, artists, and thinkers, and the West began to take notice. An Oxford professor even penned more than fifty volumes entitled *Sacred Books of the East*, which created a sensation in the West and announced that India had a special spiritual message for Europe. And Europe was listening.

As Hinduism was working on its global image and making inroads into Western thought, the Indian National Congress formed in 1885, which would lead India into its independence from Britain decades later. Muslims in India's north would also organize themselves into the Muslim League in 1906 as tensions between Hindus and Muslims grew. Soon the area of Bengal would be partitioned between the two religious groups.

All the while the world was changing. The Ottomans were overthrown in Europe. China's child emperor was ousted. And Russia's czars were toppled. In the wake of such changes Mohandas Karamchand ("Mahatma") Gandhi rose above the

Gandhi

escalating chaos in India to lead India to independence from Britain.

Gandhi's tactics of civil disobedience baffled the British. Despite Britain's new constitution in 1935 giving India power over eleven provinces, it wasn't enough, as the country's nationals chanted "Quit India!"

In 1947, Britain finally gave in and granted India her independence. The northern section of India, which was predominantly Muslim, was also allowed to create its own state, which became Pakistan. (East Pakistan would later become Bangladesh.)

From Social Organization to Social Force

As India fought for independence from Britain, another organization, besides the Muslim League, formed to rally to the cause and would later persecute those who follow religions other than Hinduism.

Benign in its name and beginnings yet radical in practice today, the Rashtriya Swayamsevel Sang, or RSS ("National Volunteers Association"), began in 1925, and assisted refugees who fled Pakistan for India soon after its independence in 1947. In 1948, Gandhi was assassinated by a former RSS member. RSS leaders were arrested and the group was banned, until it agreed to create a formal constitution.

In time the RSS changed from a social organization into a social force, advancing an ideology called *Hindutva*, meaning one common nation, one common race (under Hinduism). In reality, their aim is to purge India of anything but Hinduism, and their literature has even promoted murderous means in their purification process.

The RSS turned political with the formation of the Jan Sang Party, which later became the

Bharantiya Janata Party (BJP). As it vied for control and influence in Indian society, the group turned on those who didn't support its all-Hindu-nation agenda. In the early 1990s, RSS-inspired Hindu extremism lashed out in a hate campaign against Muslims. And in the late 1990s, the extremists refocused their rage at another group—Christians. It wasn't until an Australian missionary and his two sons were murdered by the extremists that the Hindutva agenda took center stage.

Graham Staines

He took his medical skills to help the lepers in India's Orissa state. But it was more than physical comfort that Graham Staines and his wife, Gladys, a nurse, brought to the predominantly Hindu area. They also brought the love of Christ. As they faithfully served and shared, many came to Christ and burned their Hindu idols. Hindu extremists took notice and decided the Staines family needed to be stopped.

In January 1999, Graham and his two sons, nine-year-old Philip and seven-year-old Timothy, were on a five-day evangelistic outreach away from home and decided to rest for the night in their station wagon. As they slept, militant Hindus surrounded their vehicle and set it on fire. Graham and his two sons sat huddled together in the blaze as the armed arsonists stood poised to attack them should they try to escape. Trapped, their bodies were soon consumed in the flames.

Atal Behari Vajpayee, India's Prime Minister at that time, quickly condemned the attack. Having been a founding member of the BJP, with strong ties to Hindutva extremism, Vajpayee had already proposed a law against religious conversion in India. But many condemned his proposal, seeing it merely as a means for the ruling BJP to justify the violence and deflect attention from their ideology's fanatical side.

Almost four years later, the leader of the militants as well as twelve others were convicted in an Indian court. But the leader's death sentence was later changed to life in prison and the others were acquitted.

The brutal death of Graham Staines and his sons caught the world's attention. Hindutva extremism was thrust onto center stage. And their carnage against Christians in the name of a "Hindu-only" India continued into the twenty-first century.

Persecution Continues

In 2004, the BJP lost federal control in India's elections. Partly blaming the Dalits for losing the election, the party didn't cower in their defeat but lashed out. The RSS set up a Defense Army, training young Hindu recruits to defend Hinduism and prevent Indians (especially Dalits) from

"If you are a Hindu, stay a Hindu," is written on the wall of a house in an area where people are baptized.

converting to Christianity. As of 2006, it was estimated that some three million Indians were believed to participate in the Defense Army.

The RSS oversees more than just the BJP political party and the Defense Army. It also manages a network of more than seventy Hindu groups called Sangh Parivar, which preaches that only true Indians accept and respect Hindutva. The Sangh Parivar's Bajrang Dal and Vishwa Hindu Parishad (VHP) groups are responsible for many of the recent attacks on Christians, as well as routine "reconversion" camps and ceremonies where Christian converts from Hinduism are forced to return to Hinduism. For example, in Chhattisgarh state, members of the Bajrang Dal attacked a youth prayer meeting the evening of May 3, 2009. The attackers burned Bibles and gospel tracts, broke furniture, and threatened more harm if the participants continued their Christian activities. At the time of this writing, no arrests have been made.

But one of the worst attacks on Christians occurred in August 2008 on Christians in Orissa state.

VHP leader Laxmanananda Saraswati and four of his followers were killed on August 23, 2008. But Christians didn't kill the Hindutva leader. It was a group of Maoists—atheists—who claimed responsibility for his murder. It didn't matter. The Hinduvta followers had their excuse and attacked, killing more than a hundred people, burning 4,500 homes and churches, and displacing 70,000 people, forcing many into nearby forests without food or water for days.

Hindu radicals (known by their orange head bands) prepare to destroy a Christian village.

Hindu extremists received another crushing defeat politically when the BJP lost in national and some state assembly elections in May 2009. But Christians and Hindu moderates are far from breathing a sigh of relief. India's federal government is not strong enough to curb the fanatical activities in states and regions where the radical Hindutva movement has control. Though moderate Hindus have been turned off to the Hindutva agenda, radicals try to make the world think otherwise.

Some speculate the loss in the election will not quench the flames of Hindutva fury, but only serve to foster them. As these groups use physical brutality to bully Christians into their set of beliefs, they are also using legislation to push their agenda. And it's one that stands in stark contrast to a true democracy.

CURBING THE "FORMIDABLE FORCE": INDIA'S ANTI-CONVERSION LEGISLATION

It was mid-afternoon as they gathered to pray. The rhythmic sound of voices appealing to God filled the schoolroom in Karnataka state. It was beautiful, and it was peaceful until a group of more than two dozen Hindu extremists barged into the school where they were meeting.

Beating the pastors, the Hindu attackers accused them of forcibly converting people to Christianity. But they didn't stop there. They also destroyed the Christian literature. Throwing all the Bibles and hymnals onto the floor, they set the pile on fire, and in moments the pages of Scriptures and songs were up in flames.

For nearly an hour the extremists terrorized the believers, including women. No one was free from the blows of the assailants. Finally, at four o'clock, police arrived . . . and arrested the Christians. Charged with "fraudulent conversions," the Christians were later released and the charges were dropped.

The Karnataka incident is not an isolated case. It's one of many that Christians have faced as Hindu extremists have promoted and capitalized on anti-conversion legislation. Today, five states have anti-conversion laws, some of which are dis-dainfully called "Freedom of Religion" acts. And two other states are considering such legislation.

Anti-conversion legislation is nothing new to the subcontinent. It's rooted in pre-independent India, and the motives behind such a law reek of political and fanatical religious gain under the guise of "keeping the peace" and "maintaining Hindu culture." But in reality, it's been an excuse to intimidate and propagate the Hindutva ideology.

National Loss, State Win
In British-controlled India (prior to the 1947 independence), anti-conversion legislation was unheard of, even though parts of India still under Indian rule (called "Princely States") had them. Some of these laws included the Raigarh State Conversion Act of 1936, the Patna Freedom of Religion Act of 1942, the Sarguja State Apostasy Act of 1945, and the Udaipur State Anti-Conversion Act of 1946. Other non-British areas like Bikaner, Jodhpur, Kalahandi, and Kota had similar laws with many more aimed specifically at conversions to Christianity.

After India's independence from Britain in 1947, Parliament considered a piece of legislation in 1954 called the Indian Converts Regulation and Registration Bill, which required the licensing of missionaries and the registration of converts across India, and later the Backward Communities (Religious Protection) Bill in 1960 to pre-

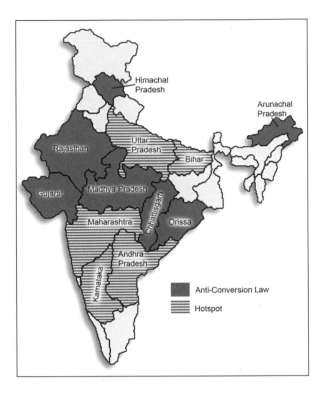

vent the conversion of Hindus to "non-Indian" religions. But without the support they needed, neither made it to law. Besides, India's constitution allows for freedom of conscience to choose one's own religion.

But these losses didn't stop proponents of anti-conversation legislation. They just changed strategies and turned their focus from the national level to the state level.

In the late 1960s, two bills successfully passed: the Orissa Freedom of Religion Act of 1967 and the Madhya Pradesh Freedom of Religion Act of 1968. Ten years later Arunachal Pradesh state followed suit with their "Freedom of Religion Act" that prohibited the conversion from one religious faith to another by use of force or inducement or by fraudulent means. Decades later the state of Tamil Nadu passed a "Prohibition of Forcible Conversion of Religion Ordinance" in 2002.

Now a publicly known offense, these laws specified that cruelty and purposeful intent to hurt the "sentiments" of others is a penal offense punishable by imprisonment and fines. But in the four decades since these laws have been on the books, no one has been convicted of such a crime. So, what's the point of such laws?

Disturbing the Social Structure

As early as the Orissa Act in the 1960s, the proponents' intent was obvious. Forcible conversion isn't the concern. It is conversion to any religion other than Hinduism.

Even prior to the Orissa Act, Hindu Law enactments in the 1950s were aimed at keeping low-caste Hindus within the fold of Hinduism. If low-caste Hindus leave their position, it disrupts the Hindu caste order that upholds the status of higher castes, like the Brahmin. Hindus believe low-castes received that fate because of past sins in their previous incarnation—"bad kharma." So their low-caste status is their payment for the wrongs they committed in their previous lives. Christianity upsets their view. Hindus believe God created man unequal. Christianity doesn't.

The lower castes could also be considered the "backbone" of the country, performing menial labor and tasks, such as farming and cleaning, that a high-caste Hindu would never consider. So when a Dalit, an untouchable, converts from Hinduism to Christianity, he leaves behind more than his religion. He is leaving behind his low-caste status so that higher castes can no longer control him.

But not every Hindu in India is for the anti-conversion legislation, which is contrary to what Hindutva extremists want the world to believe. Many moderate Hindus have promoted India's Reservation System, which is somewhat of a quota system reserving positions in the government and education for low-caste nationals. Others have noted how helping the untouchables has disrupted the Hindu caste order: "Recently, indiscriminate terrors and persecution have been unleashed on Indian Christians because they are helping the untouchable and poor to get rid of the caste system, ignorance and poverty....Christians and missionaries in India are opposed particularly when they help India's aboriginals who were forced to become the 'lower castes.' In fact, all who try to help the downtrodden are opposed by the 'upper castes.'"[21]

Opponents of anti-conversion legislation see this trend ever increasing as large numbers of Dalits turn to Christ. In fact, a majority of Christian conversions are happening among the Dalits, more so than among the upper castes, with more than seventy percent of all Christians from Dalit and tribal communities.

Some also view anti-conversion laws as a means to force the masses to accept humiliating conditions without protest. They also view conversion as a way for those in low castes to protest their status and have a life of dignity and hope through Jesus Christ—something they can't obtain as a low-caste Hindu. Once a low-caste Hindu, always a low-caste Hindu, unless one converts. Ironically (and hypocritically), these laws have prohibited conversions from Hinduism, but reconversion back to Hinduism is acceptable. In fact, if a Hindu becomes a Christian, Hindu extremists call it a "conversion." But if a Christian decides to become a Hindu, they use the word "homecoming."

And it is this perceived "betrayal" to Hinduism and the caste system that has fueled the anti-conversion legislation and heated debates.

---

21 Mangalwadi, p. xviii.

Inflammatory Rhetoric

Arguments for and against the anti-conversion legislation abound. On one end of the spectrum, proponents say the laws are needed to promote peace and stability: "In a predominantly Hindu society, a large-scale conversion...generates and fosters a rift in the society and leads a stable society into a disintegrated society. It disturbs the social structure and leads to a class of cultures...."[22] Another argument is cultural preservation with the Hindutva ideology of a "Hindu-only" society. Conversion "of Hindus to Christianity or Islam has a tendency to disturb the local custom and faith as well as indigenous institutions."[23]

Anti-conversion supporters have gone so far as labeling any Christian missions as an outside foreign body bent on "conquering" the subcontinent by means of helping the lower castes through education and medicine. Those siding with anti-conversion laws have labeled Christians as "formidable forces" and have argued, "Globally supported and funded Christian missions are functioning with unabated zeal and enthusiasm to spread their tentacles to find out victims for conversions to Christianity."[24]

Many are seeing through the inflammatory rhetoric and appeals for "debates on religious

---

22 Venugopal.

23 Ibid.

24 Ibid.

Radicals torched the church building

conversion" as a ploy to promote the political ideology of Hindutva. After the August 2008 mass attack on Christians in Orissa state, causing more than a hundred deaths and seventy thousand to flee their homes, the RSS-supported VHP (World Council of Hindus) called for a debate on conversions. Knowing a Moaist claimed responsibility for killing the VHP leader, which spurred the attacks, why would the VHP call for such a debate? When an atheist group takes responsibility for killing a Hindutva leader yet the Christians are blamed, the situation is not only paradoxical but irrational. Therefore, what would more rhetoric accomplish except to divert attention from the true nature of the crime and to promote such extremist ideology?

Another argument for anti-conversion legislation is a disingenuous concern for lower castes being taken advantage of by Christians. In substance, such proponents are saying, "We're looking out for you." Though some have noted odd reasons for low-caste Hindus converting to Christianity, their "concern" comes across more patronizing and offensive, in effect saying, "We don't think you're intelligent enough to make a decision about changing your religion."

Throughout the debate, the media hasn't helped matters, suggesting that conversions are at the root of the ongoing violence in India. And as the finger is pointed at Christian converts, the Hindu extremists who are instigating the violence

Hindu extremists burned more than 400 churches in Orissa in August 2008.

are not being held responsible. However, not all Hindu extremists are getting off scot-free. Police arrested BJP candidate Ashok Sahu after he delivered an inflammatory speech accusing Radhakant Nayak (a member of the Congress Party), Archbishop Raphael Cheenath, and missionaries of plotting the murder of Laxmananda Saraswati that led to the August 2008 Orissa attacks.

More Accusations, More Glory
As the debate continues and other states consider anti-conversion laws, Hindu extremists will use the laws as an excuse to attack Christians. In Tamil Nadu state, members of the RSS interrupted the screening of the *JESUS* film and accused the pastor of forcible conversions in May 2009. That same month in Madhya Pradesh state, Pastor Ramesh Mandevey was attacked by Hindu extremists, after they lodged a complaint with the police accusing him of forcibly converting Hindus.

Some Hindu extremists have been less than covert in their motives for attacking Christians, and their methods give new meaning to "forcible conversions," such as with Laxmananda Saraswati before he was murdered by Maoists in August 2008. An armed mob of 400 Hindu extremists ransacked churches, homes, and buildings in Orissa's Kandhamal district in December 2007. Many pastors and believers fled to a nearby forest to escape death. When the extremists hunted down the famished Christians, they coerced them to embrace Hinduism in exchange for food and shelter. At knife-point extremists shaved the heads of many and then forced them to bow to Hindu idols. After police investigated the attack, Saraswati told the media, "The attacks were because of conversions to Christianity in the region."

Even former Hindu extremists who turn to Jesus have been accused of using coercion to lead others to Christ. A man named Vasant, who used to persecute Christians in the name of Hindutva, was targeted in a pamphlet circulated by Hindu extremists: "This man who belonged to a family of Brahmin priests, who has now, being influenced by the 'English,' begun to convert a lot of people through deception, which includes, according to his detractors, 'speaking kindly to the poor, helping them in all ways, finding jobs for the young men, finding good grooms for young women and arranging for their marriage,' etc., all with a view to 'converting' them. Oh Hindu brothers, if at all you have any masculinity in you, unite and see that you finish off this man."

But the glory lies in Vasant's response: "I tell them about the gospel because they do not know the truth. They should know Jesus died for them and they should be saved." To him, showing kindness and helping the poor are not forcing conversion. It's simply showing Christ's love.

Christians who take the Great Commandment and the Great Commission seriously are what threaten the Hindutva agenda. Such demonstration of Christ's love is disturbing the social order in India—that is, the fanatical Hindu social order based on the caste system. And as Hindus continue turning to Christ, extremists will step up efforts to stop them ... unless, of course they, too, turn to Christ, like Vasant.

INDIA TODAY:
A FANATIC FINDS FREEDOM

The following is the testimony of Narayan Gowda, a former leader of a radical Hindu gang and persecutor of Christians. Now, he glorifies God by serving Him and His persecuted Body.

I was taken to Hindutva training camps. [The teachers] encouraged us to use violence against anyone who did not subscribe to their idea of the Hindu nation.

We were told by our mentors in the RSS that we could do anything we wanted without fear because, "We are behind you." Every time we did some brave exploits like intimidating or beating up some unarmed Christian preacher or group of Muslims, we were treated like heroes.

We became tremendously unpopular with the local police officials because they were never able to make any charges stick.

One day, my RSS mentors showed me a small brick building... near Bangalore. This was where a pastor had constructed a place of worship with contributions from his flock—mostly poor migrant workers. I was told to break it down and kill the pastor and his family. My gang and I had often threatened the pastor as he worked among the poor in that place.

We chose a dark night and went to this shed. We used hammers, pickaxes, and other metal tools [to tear down the shed]. Then we went to look for the pastor and his family. Providentially, the pastor had sent his family away on a visit, and he was at an all-night prayer meeting.

When he was informed of the demolition, the pastor rushed to the ruins. A police officer met him and urged him to name anyone he suspected. The pastor knew we had done it, but he refused to name us. He gave a statement in writing that he did not charge anyone with the crime, and that he had prayed for their forgiveness. The police officer begged, pleaded, and even threatened, but the pastor was unmoved.

The church decided to get together and pray for the gang...immediately.

One day my mother, a Hindu, took ill and was rushed to the hospital. While [there], the chaplain gave her a book—the New Testament. My mother took the New Testament home with her when she was discharged, believing it to be a holy book.

A few days later, I went home. Even as I was taking off my shoes, my eyes fell on this strange black book with a cross on it! I demanded she explain why she had brought this book home. During my visit, I picked up the book and read it a few times. I found a new kind of peace in my heart.

I went to the hospital one day and asked to see the chaplain. Upon seeing me, alarm jumped into his eyes. He had heard of my anti-Christian sentiments and thought I had come to pick a quarrel with him! I assured him it was not so and I wanted to learn more about the Bible. But he was not eager to talk to me. He invited me to attend the service in the church at the hospital on Sunday morning.

On Sunday morning, I left for the church at the hospital. It was a new experience and hard to put into words. The whole large gathering sang songs and praised God together; they prayed and worshiped. A peace stole into my heart that morning.

That week I went back to my friends. Everybody began to talk of the change in me, how I had become quiet, silent, calm, and no longer violent.

Things changed for me at home. The same mother who prayed to the gods to change me was not able to accept my changed life [as a Christian]. She said I had been brainwashed, that I had lost my mind.

The neighbors who lived on our street also showed their disapproval. As I would walk past them, they said loud critical comments about people who had given up the gods of their ancestors and now prayed to the gods of the outcastes and untouchables. In spite of the persecution, I did not leave home, nor did I go back to my old friends. Then one day, I was thrown out of my house and had to take refuge in the homes of Christians.

I went to the police station to meet the assistant commissioner of the police in my area. The same man had been an inspector when I was active as a local tough. He could not believe I was the same person who had been such a headache to the entire police force of the city! I thought he would now take the opportunity to pay me back for the numerous times I had harassed him and caused him trouble, by lashing me. But he came and stood in front of me, laid a hand on my shoulder and said, "Mr. Narayan Gowda, your Yesu Christu [Jesus Christ] has done what the entire police force and the laws of this country could not do—He has changed you into a law-abiding citizen. I have closed the files against you. You are a free man. You can go!"

Sometimes I share the same pulpit as the dear pastor whose life and family I had threatened and whose church I had demolished. The joy that fills my life cannot be explained in words as I share my testimony and give the gospel. All praise and glory be to God!

FUTURE GLORY:
PRAY FOR INDIA

"Lord, your friend Lazarus is very sick," said the messenger to Jesus as he looked into the solemn face that hinted at sadness.

"The point of his sickness is not death, but My Father's glory," He responded, "so that I will be glorified through this as well."

Perhaps Jesus was already anticipating the great disappointment of Lazarus' sisters, Mary and Martha, when they heard He wasn't coming. At least not yet.

Days passed before Jesus finally decided to see Lazarus. "It's time to go to Judea," He said.

But His disciples were fear-stricken. "Master, the Jews in Judea wanted to stone You," they objected. "How could You go back there?"

After clarifying the confusion that Lazarus was surely dead, not just sleeping, He told them why they needed to go. "This will be another chance for you to believe in Me," He said.

Just as soon as He uttered to His disciples, "Let's go," one of His followers made a surprising plea.

"Let's go too—and die with Him!"

That man was Thomas. Though perhaps perceived as impulsive, he was still ready to die with Christ.

So they departed. When they arrived, Jesus met a mix of emotions.

"If You would have been here," said Mary, "my brother would still be alive!"

And some of the Jews who grieved with Mary and Martha argued, "He healed a blind man, so why couldn't He keep Lazarus from dying?"

The stone in front of Lazarus' tomb was rolled away. But it wasn't the smell of a decaying body that poured out. It was Lazarus that walked out. The crowd of mourners was astonished.

Many of the Jewish leaders who had witnessed this miracle believed Jesus was the promised Messiah. But others went to the Pharisees and reported what they had seen.

The chief priests and Pharisees convened. They needed to decide what to do with this man who performed miracles.

"If we leave Him alone, the entire nation will follow Him!" argued one. "Then the Romans will come and take away our power and nation."

"You don't know anything!" said Caiaphas, the high priest, his voice rising over the hushed murmur. "Why should the whole nation perish because of Him? Let Him die for all the people!"

From that time on, the Jews plotted Jesus' death.

* * *

Like the apostle Thomas, many Christ followers in India today are saying, "Let us also go, that we may die with Him" (John 11:16), as they willingly suffer for Him through beatings, imprisonment, and loss of possessions. For some, that means death. Most new converts have left behind a religion with no hope, a life that restricted them to the bottom of the social caste, confining them to a life where they are told they are "untouchable" and a "pollutant."

As they become freed from the deeply embedded lies of kharma and reincarnation, they are upsetting a social order that has plagued India for thousands of years, surviving foreign occupiers and Western colonies. And like the Jews who witnessed Lazarus' resurrection from the dead, Hindu extremists are noticing and plotting against these believers who have dared to disturb their social structure and threaten their high-caste status.

Using anti-conversion laws to intimidate and inflame an already tense situation, Hindu fanatics are stopping at nothing to keep their caste system in place. They've raided prayer meetings and beaten the attendees. They've launched charges of forcible conversions against Christians. They've gunned down believers on the streets. They've burned down churches. And they've tonsured, or shaved the heads, of believers who refuse to convert back to Hinduism. (Tonsuring is illegal in India.) At times they've been successful. Some have converted back to Hinduism. Thankfully, most have not.

As we read these accounts, we are not helpless. We can pray for our brothers and sisters in

India's "untouchables" gather to worship the Lord.

Christ in India. We can ask God that new believers will be well-grounded in God's Word so they can stand strong when faced with persecution. We can pray the world will see the true fanatical side of the Hindutva agenda. We can ask God to encourage those Christians whose church buildings have been torn down by fanatics, and that they will find ways to gather and worship. And we can pray for those Christians who have been driven from their homes and lost all they owned. Most importantly, we can pray that they boldly proclaim the gospel of Jesus Christ, and that God will open the eyes of the Indians to the One who is Truth itself.

We can also give practical help. For decades, The Voice of the Martyrs has been assisting persecuted Christians in India. Through gifts to the ministry, VOM has relocated the widows of martyred pastors and helped them learn a trade to support their families. Pastors have been given legal assistance when arrested for their Christian witness and have also been provided with ministry tools such as bicycles, Bibles, and literature. Churches have been rebuilt after they were destroyed by fanatical Hindus, and Bibles have been printed in several languages of India and distributed into the hands of those who are seeking Truth.

As you reach the end of this book, remember that India's tale of glory hasn't ended. It continues as Christians are refusing to deny Christ in the face of intimidation and torture...and as Hindu fanatics turn to Christ. Their tales of glory have only just begun. And you can be a part of them, too. Will you?

FOR FURTHER READING

The following books and resources were consulted in the writing of this book. However, The Voice of the Martyrs and the author do not necessarily share the views presented in every resource.

Edwardes, Stephen Meredyth and Herbert Leonard Offley Garrett. *Mughal Rule in India* (New Delhi: Atlantic Publishers & Distributors, 1995).

Fenger, Johannes Ferdinand and Emil Fancke, trans. *History of the Tranquebar Mission* (Tranquebar: Evangelical Lutheran Mission Press, 1863).

Huc, M. L'Abbé. *Christianity in China, Tartary, and Thibet, Volume I* (London: Longman, Brown, Green, Longmans, & Roberts, 1857).

James, M. R., editor and translator. *The New Testament Apocrypha* (Berkeley, CA: The Apocryphile Press, 2004).

Johnstone, Patrick. *Operation World*. <www.operationworld.org/country/indi/owtext.html>. Last modified November 2, 2008. Accessed October 16, 2009.

Kaye, Sir John William. *Christianity in India: An Historical Narrative* (London: Smith, Elder and Co., 1859).

Mangalwadi, Vishal. *The Quest for Freedom and Dignity: Caste, Conversion and Cultural Revolu-*

tion (South Asian Resources: GLS Publishing, 2001).

Moffett, Samuel Hugh. *A History of Christianity in Asia, Volume I: Beginnings to 1500* (Maryknoll, NY: Orbis Books, 1998).

Moffett, Samuel Hugh. *A History of Christianity in Asia, Volume II: 1500 to 1900* (Maryknoll, NY: Orbis Books, 2005).

Monier-Williams, Monier. *Religious Thought and Life in India: Part I, Vedism, Brahmanism, and Hinduism* (London: John Murray, 1885).

Morris, John Hughes. *History of the Welsh Calvinistic Methodist Foreign Mission to the Year End 1904* (New Delhi: Indus Publishing Company, 1996).

Neill, Stephen. *A History of Christianity in India: The Beginnings to A.D. 1707* (New York: Cambridge University Press, 1984).

Philips, Cyril Henry and Patrick Tuck, ed. *The East India Company 1784–1834* (New York: Routledge, 1998).

Richter, Julius. *A History of Missions in India* (New York: Fleming H. Revell Company, 1908).

Sinharaja, Tammita-Delgoda. *A Traveller's History of India*, Second Edition (Brooklyn, NY: Interlink Books, 1999).

Smith, George. *A Short History of Christian Missions* (Edinburgh: T & T Clark, 1884).

Venugopal, Dr. Justice P. "Why Anti-Conversion Law Needed" <www.hvk.org/articles/0503/135.html>. Posted May 11, 2003. Accessed October 21, 2009.

Walsh, J. *A Memorial of the Futtehgurh Mission and Her Martyred Missionaries* (Philadelphia: Joseph M. Wilson, 1859).

Other Resources
Warrior Empire: The Lost World of India's Most Powerful Dynasty: The Mughal DVD (Yap Films for History Television Network Productions, 2006).

The Voice of the Martyrs monthly newsletter and Web site: www.persecution.com.

RESOURCES

The Voice of the Martyrs has many books, videos, brochures, and other products to help you learn more about the persecuted church. In the U.S., to order materials or receive our free monthly newsletter, call (800) 747-0085 or write to:

The Voice of the Martyrs
P.O. Box 443
Bartlesville, OK 74005-0443
www.persecution.com
thevoice@vom-usa.org

If you are in Australia, Canada, New Zealand, South Africa, or the United Kingdom, contact:

Australia:
Voice of the Martyrs
P.O. Box 250
Lawson NSW 2783
Australia

Website: www.persecution.com.au
Email: thevoice@persecution.com.au

Canada:
Voice of the Martyrs, Inc.
P.O. Box 608
Streetsville, ON L5M 2C1
Canada

Website: www.persecution.net
Email: thevoice@vomcanada.org

New Zealand:

Voice of the Martyrs
P.O. Box 5482
Papanui, Christchurch 8542
New Zealand

Website: www.persecution.co.nz
Email: thevoice@persecution.co.nz

South Africa:

Christian Mission International
P.O. Box 7157
1417 Primrose Hill
South Africa

Email: cmi@icon.co.za

United Kingdom:

Release International
P.O. Box 54
Orpington BR5 9RT
United Kingdom

Website: www.releaseinternational.org
Email: info@releaseinternational.org